I Hope We
Never Meet

I Hope We Never Meet

CLIENT STORIES *of* TRAGEDY, RECOVERY, *and* ACCOUNTABILITY FROM *a* LIFE *in* DETERRENCE LAW

ANDREW FINKELSTEIN, ESQ.

with

SARAH LUNHAM

LIONCREST
PUBLISHING

I HOPE WE NEVER MEET

Client Stories of Tragedy, Recovery, and Accountability
from a Life in Deterrence Law

ISBN	978-1-5445-2404-7	*Hardcover*
	978-1-5445-2403-0	*Paperback*
	978-1-5445-2402-3	*Ebook*

This book is dedicated to all the hard-working people in my office who collaborated with me on these and so many other cases. Your caring, compassion, and concern for our community and clients inspire me every day.

Contents

Introduction

Odds are, I'm very sorry you're reading my book.

Many of my years-long relationships with clients start with the same regret. As a personal injury lawyer, I often meet people in the middle of the worst days of their lives. Nobody who comes into my office for the first time is happy to be there, but I'm always glad to meet them—across my desk or by their hospital beds. I take no pleasure in the grief and shock they're experiencing, but I know (as you'll see in the stories of loss and recovery I share in this book) that they are part of a larger narrative. There's something heroic about every one of them, even beyond the strength it takes to tell me about what's just happened to redirect their lives in a direction they never wanted or planned.

No matter who they are, and although we've just met, I already know a few things about these people (as I suspect I do about you). For one, I know there's hope. From my outsider's perspective and years of experience, I know the person I'm speaking with is living through the worst days of their lives. And I know that things *will* get better. There's no room left to get worse.

If they're talking to me in my professional capacity, I also know someone has told them they need to consult a lawyer. During their struggle to go on without a loved one they've lost or in the face of a grueling physical recovery, they're talking to me because they want to right a wrong. They want to do this, not for themselves, but to hold the system that's responsible to account and to protect other people from harm. They're thinking about taking on the hero's work of standing against injustice, but they're also feeling overwhelmed, guilty, or unsure. I always grieve for them and with them, but I'm always awed by them as well. And proud to stand with them.

I tell them that it's my objective to ensure that, as time goes on, they'll look back on our meeting as the absolute worst time because, I hope, it will mark a turning point where things began to get just a fraction better. I tell them I've been right here where we are far too many times but that I've seen what comes next, and it does—it *will*—get better. Not every day is better than the one before, and it never gets easy, but there is hope, and they're not alone.

If you're reading this book because you're living through tragedy, please know that you have my genuine and experience-informed sympathy. You also have my respect. I hope you'll take some of my hope as well.

When I first meet with people, they are entirely and understandably overwhelmed. They don't know how to go forward. They don't know what they should do or how to do it. Often, in addition to the practical and emotional upheaval they're facing, serious financial worries threaten them. Finally, they're struggling with ethical questions: How could this have happened? Who's responsible? What can and should I do about it?

My advice to them and you is always the same: do what you need to do to take care of yourself and your family. If you want to stand up to those responsible, you don't have to do anything about it right now. That's what I'm there for. I have a team of investigators and experts ready to determine what happened, which system failed, and where the blame belongs. The process can begin operating in the background while their thoughts, focus, and whatever energy they have left can go to taking care of themselves and their family. I promise that I'll take care of who did this. Then, I tell them a story of someone I've worked with who faced something similar.

I tell these stories for several reasons: because thinking about something else, even for a few minutes, is a kind of respite; because I've seen how people take inspiration and hope from hearing about someone who faced something equally unthinkable and came out the other side; and because from the distance of time or another person's life, it's easier to see that there is, in fact, a story.

They are living a story that's unique to them but also universal to everyone who's survived tragedy. They are at the beginning of a journey no one has ever wanted to take, and it helps them to know that it will have a middle and, eventually, an end—even if the effects of it last the rest of their lives.

Sadly, I've had enough experience that I've seen one that's similar no matter what their situation. Because I'm not there to tailor a story for you, I've grouped the nine I've collected for this book into two sections—wrongful death and catastrophic injury. Here, I'll provide a few details to help you select the one that's closest to your situation.

- Chapter 1: The death of a seventy-two-year-old man who would not have died trying to stop the sexual assault of his seventy-year-old wife had the owners of their building provided the exterior lighting and security they'd promised.

- Chapter 2: The death of a twenty-seven-year-old man killed by a tire thrown from a company's inadequately maintained truck.

- Chapter 3: The death of a six-year-old child run over by a utility company repair truck.

- Chapter 4: The death of a thirty-nine-year-old husband and father caused by his workplace's refusal to install an inexpensive piece of safety equipment.

- Chapter 5: The death of an eighty-year-old nursing home patient from infected bedsores.

- Chapter 6: A delivery driver who lost his leg when his company-owned box truck rear-ended another truck on the highway.

- Chapter 7: A man left paralyzed from the neck down when an improperly affixed toilet seat shot out from under him.

- Chapter 8: The traumatic brain injury suffered by a woman whose bicycle hit a broken speed bump.

- Chapter 9: A young man living with chronic pain after falling down an elevator shaft.

These are all true stories of people I worked with over the years in which they survived, recovered, found meaning, and built new lives. I've changed identifying details to protect their privacy, but they're "real life" enough, I trust, to offer you some hope and provide a bit of a roadmap for the journey you've been forced onto. If you're reading this book for inspiration, I suggest finding the story most similar to yours and starting there. If you're reading to get a broader picture of how these stories develop as legal cases and move through the process of litigation,[1] you can read the book sequentially to follow the larger story.

My part in this story starts, as most people's stories do, with my parents. My mom and dad were both extraordinary people. Mom lost her mother when she was just seventeen, but she didn't let it stop her. She went to college, where she met my dad and didn't slow down when she had kids.

I was one of three boys and remember tagging along (and later being dragged) to her bowling league and to rehearsals for pretty much any musical you can think of because our babysitters rarely came back for a second engagement. We were a lot to handle. But Mom managed us and made it look easy. She was tough, but she was also incredibly loving to us and, I found out later, to many, many others.

I've never been to a bigger funeral or heard so many stories of small, impactful kindnesses. Hearing how many lives she touched inspired the family to set up a charity in her name: the Diane Finkelstein Fund for Families in Crisis. Like Mom, it gives money to people who need a little help to get through a tough time in their lives. We've covered everything from car repairs to a month's rent (and all proceeds from the sale of this book will go to further its work).

---

1 "Litigation" simply means taking legal action–it's taking somebody to court or suing them.

Dad outlived my mother by twenty-five years. Happily, I didn't have to wait until his funeral to see the impact he had on people's lives. I still remember the day it hit home for me. It was the first time he let me sit "up front" in his car.

Every year, he took me to the spring carnival at a high school thirty miles away, and every year, I lobbied to sit in the front seat. The carnival was a fundraiser, and his refusal was as predictable as the nice couple—a teacher and her husband—who found Dad at some point while we were there. They would come up to us by the Ferris wheel or at the popcorn stand and talk to Dad for a while.

Usually, I got bored and wandered around nearby. When Dad caught up with me again, there were always tears in his eyes. I didn't think that much about it. It was just one of those things that happened at the carnival, like paying for everything with long strings of red tickets. Besides, it wasn't that unusual. For as long as I can remember, people have approached my dad in restaurants or at the gas station to shake his hand. They always talked in low voices that carried the kind of suppressed adult emotion that embarrasses kids.

That year, I remember thinking I was too grown-up for rinky-dink fairs. Dad was talking to the couple I only knew as "Jennifer's parents." (I only knew that because the whole Saturday was called the Jennifer's Day Fair.) I had drifted off to watch the kiddie coaster—a rickety track that unfolded from the back of a trailer—when I spotted an older kid standing there doing the same thing. Every go-round, he'd wave at his little sister squealing in one of the little cars. I strolled over. "Pretty dumb, right?" I suggested.

The kid didn't even turn his head to look at me. "What do you know?" he said in the way only teenagers can dismiss younger kids.

"I just get bored babysitting sometimes," I said. "I thought…"

The kid relaxed. "Oh," he said. "Yeah. It's just—I won the scholarship this year. It isn't dumb to me."

"Me either," I said. "I just meant the ride. Like *this* is a roller coaster?"

"Right?" He looked at me then with a grin. "My kid sister…"

He stopped talking, watching something over my shoulder. I turned and saw Dad, still standing with Jennifer's parents, waving me over.

"Gotta go," I said, half relieved, half embarrassed.

"That's your dad?"

"Yeah." I looked down at the tickets in my hand. No way this kid was here with his dad. "Anyway, congratulations on the scholarship."

He held out his hand, and I shook it like we were men. "Thanks," he said, but he was still looking at Dad.

On the way back to the car, I asked Dad what a scholarship was and which game let you win one. Dad looked at me for an intense moment, then said I could sit up front. I was old enough to hear about Jennifer.

She'd been eight years old and in her mom's car on the way to school when a New Jersey Transit Authority bus, swerving to avoid a car that hadn't stopped at a stop sign, crossed into the opposite lane and hit Jennifer's. The medics got her out of the car and to the hospital, but she'd died there.

The teachers at Jennifer's elementary and at the high school where her mom and dad taught held a fundraiser to help cover the funeral costs and the mother's medical bills. They said all they could think about was how much Jenny would have loved the rides.

"That little girl's death and everything it put her parents and the other teachers and students through should never have happened," Dad said. "The transit authority hadn't bothered looking into the backgrounds of the people it hired as drivers, and it didn't train them well. When their drivers caused crashes, they didn't do more than reprimand them. They said it took too much time, so they just looked the other way. They didn't care enough about the lives of people like Jennifer and her family to do more. They just wanted those buses to run cheaply and on time."

There was passion in Dad's voice—serious and focused—and it frightened me a little.

"Jennifer's parents wanted to protect the other people in their school district from having the same thing happen again. They knew the only way to make the transit authority take action was to hit it where it put all its priority—its income."

"And you were their lawyer," I guessed.

Dad nodded. "There are two doors into the courtroom, Andrew. Most people only ever see the big front door that swings open for companies and government agencies that can afford all the lawyers they want. But there's a smaller, person-sized door. It's every bit as heavy as the big one, but when one of the big guys does something very wrong, brave people can go through the other door and get justice. Jennifer's parents did that, and it cost the transit authority a lot of money. Now it does a better job hiring and training its drivers, not because it developed a conscience, but because it learned it's cheaper to take reasonable precautions than to risk having what happened to Jennifer happen again."

"You helped her parents make it expensive for them?" I asked.

He nodded.

"And that's what pays for the carnival?"

"Basically," Dad said. "Every year, Jennifer's parents throw a party for all the people who could have just as easily been the ones the bus killed. They bring in all of Jennifer's favorite rides on trailers, and they invite everyone to add their five-dollar tickets to the fund that will send another kid to college just like Jennifer would have gone to college one day. That's the scholarship. It's a way of making something good come out of the worst thing that could happen to a parent."

I saw him glance to make sure my seatbelt was on, and we drove the rest of the way home without talking. I never forgot about the courtroom's two doors, and I kept going back to the festival with Dad every year. I figured if Jennifer never got too old for it, neither would I.

But I didn't start planning to be a lawyer. Dad wanted me to, and he made no secret about it, but I went to college for business and did a double major in finance and marketing. I got a job right out of school at a brokerage house, exactly like I'd planned, and I hated it, which wasn't the plan at all.

I wanted to go back to school for an MBA, but Dad wanted me to go to law school. I was debating between the two when I happened to meet a billionaire. Never one to miss the chance to learn something, I asked him what he thought I should do. He told me the best education he'd gotten was in law school and that in his experience (which was considerable), the best CEOs had law degrees, not MBAs. I went to law school.

Law school is an incredible education in many things, and for me, one of those things was my dad. It was there that I understood for the first time why he loved what he did and why he had always thought I should be a lawyer too. For me—for us—there is no more worthwhile life's work than to work with people in pursuit of justice.

I'd wanted to go into business because I loved people. I love talking, listening, and working together with people. It's what you do in business, but it's also, I discovered, what you do in law. The big difference is the reason why you do it. In business, you do it for money. In law, you do it for ideas—ideas like justice and deterrence and protecting the little guy.

The old-fashioned name for a lawyer is "counselor at law," and that's what I do. I listen, and I counsel people about the law. Wanting to share stories that offer hope to anyone facing the kind of heartache I've seen so many of my inspiring clients overcome was my first reason for writing this book. I also hope to provide some measure of counseling here.

While each chapter tells the story of one remarkable person's journey through the most challenging time of their life, it's also part of a larger story. That narrative tells how cases are developed and move through the legal system and what those cases mean for our shared democracy and individual safety.

I'll explain why each of these stories is a David-and-Goliath story and why juries are the guardians of a community's values. I'll talk you through how I support my clients with investigators, experts, animations, and focus groups, and how we sue to cause changes that improve safety for everyone.

I'm a deterrence lawyer—I help my clients stop companies from hurting other people the way they've been hurt. And I'm a doorstop; I hold open my father's second, smaller courtroom door for people who are willing to come in and take on a Goliath. I'll start with one—a woman named Ottie—whom I met when my father died.

CHAPTER 1

Value Every Life

When Ottie Lewis sent her daughter out of my office with one arched eyebrow, it surprised me. Ella was no shrinking daisy, and I knew what had happened to Ottie. I had expected she'd want her daughter's support. But Ella left, and Ottie sank back into her chair. I didn't say anything. She could take her time.

Ottie was a few years younger than my dad, and I'd just come back to Newburgh, New York, after spending a beautiful, bright fall weekend with him. Dad was eighty and in decent health, but, as he would have put it, he wasn't getting any younger. I'd been grateful for the weekend with him. It was time Ella hadn't had with her dad. He'd been killed in his apartment the month before. She'd come in last week and told me the story, and now she was back with her mother. Ottie had been sharp-witted and light with her daughter. Now, she sat heavily in my office chair like she held a terrible and invisible weight in her lap.

"It was my fault," she said. "I picked that apartment complex. I knew it wasn't in the safest neighborhood, but it was what we could afford, and it was close to Joe's work. He had to get up so early in the morning to take the bus from our old place. I wanted him to get that extra hour of sleep every day. I looked in the newspapers, and I found that place. Joe and I went to take a look at it. We knew it wasn't a safe area, but it wasn't any worse than where we'd been living, and it did have security. The building manager toured us around, showed us the video cameras they had up and the lights that came on at night, and how the gate into the place was always locked. He said they had a security guard they paid for themselves. I felt good about that. I trusted the man."

Her voice trailed off, and she looked down at her hands, twisting a tissue in her lap.

"What happened next, Mrs. Lewis?" I asked her.

"Call me Ottie." She waved the tissue at me. "Everybody does, and no, it's not short for Dottie before you ask. My baby cousin couldn't say 'auntie,' and I've been everybody's auntie ever since. Don't you try to be different."

"Alright," I said. "I'd be honored."

Her nod seemed to say that was as it should be. Going back to the question I'd asked, she explained, "We moved in. And pretty soon after, we figured out that security guard they were bragging about walked our building and seven others at night. We hardly ever saw him. Then the light by the gate burned out, and people started propping it open. I complained to the manager a few times, and Joe called the company that owned the whole place, but nothing changed, and we kind of gave up because they didn't seem to care. I shouldn't have, but you get used to things, you know?"

I nodded. I did know. We often brought human factors experts in to help juries understand how people interact with different environments. They could explain the science behind it, but Ottie was exactly right in her assessment.

"It wasn't your fault," I told her. "Our brains are programmed by evolution to stop noticing things that don't change."

"Makes sense," she said. "If it's not changing, it's not a lion stalking you, right?" She chuckled, but her smile dissolved almost instantly. "Just as deadly," she said. Her eyes had gone blank. "I'd almost rather…"

Then she told me what had happened.

The man must have been waiting for her in the dark stairwell because he seemed just to appear. She'd been carrying shopping bags, and it took her a minute to get the apartment door unlocked, but as soon as she opened it, he was there, crashing in behind her—his hand over her mouth. He'd kicked the door shut and pinned her against the wall before she knew what was happening.

"I realized I was still holding the shopping bags," she said. "I let them go, but I couldn't get my one hand free. I did get a big fistful of his hair with my other hand. Couldn't pull his head away from me, though. I started yelling, but he put a sock in my mouth, and I remember thinking, *An old woman like me? He—*

I stopped her. She didn't need to go over it all again. She'd told the police everything, and I had read the report. The man physically and sexually assaulted Ottie until her husband came home and found them.

"Joe was never a big guy, but he was scrappy." Ottie shook her head. "Got killed trying to save me. I just wish—"

She couldn't go on. She held up her hand, signaling me to wait. "I just wish he hadn't seen me like that. And how am I supposed to hold my head up now? My children and my grandchildren, all their cousins and my neighbors, everyone I'm an auntie to—and that's a lot of people—how am I going to look at them knowing they're thinking about what got done to me?"

Ottie trailed off. When she spoke again, she looked haunted. "We were planning our fiftieth wedding anniversary. Instead, I planned his funeral."

Trust, Vulnerability, and Betrayal

Ottie's trust in the apartment complex made her vulnerable to the predator who beat her, raped her, and killed her husband. If the company had provided the security they promised, Ottie wouldn't have been attacked, and Joe would still be alive.[2] But they betrayed Ottie's trust, and she felt guilty for having believed them. Of course, she wasn't at fault. Trust is foundational to society. Without it, we couldn't eat anything we didn't grow, take prescription medications, or drive on a highway with other cars and trucks. Like Ottie, we trust that when people make promises about our safety, they'll keep them.

We trust the companies that built our homes to design them to keep out rain and wind. We trust the pipes aren't full of lead or the walls riddled with mold. We trust the cleaning products we use not to kill us, and the appliances we buy not to catch fire. That trust is based, in part, on faith in our fellow humans,

---

2 These are called "wrongful death cases" because the death shouldn't have happened, i.e., it was wrongful. It could and should have been prevented.

but also in the confidence that if they betray our trust, there's a system that will hold them accountable.

Every chapter in this book tells the story of a person like Ottie who stood up to a wrongdoer when their reasonably placed trust was violated. To me, this is heroic. We all make ourselves vulnerable every day, and it's often arbitrary who gets hurt when companies aren't as concerned about the safety of others as they claim to be. Ottie and Joe were random victims of a crime, but the crime was not random. The crime rate at Ottie and Joe's building was seven times higher than the surrounding area—burned-out security lights and one guard spread between seven buildings create an easy environment for crime—but of course, Ottie's landlord had never mentioned this. When I told her about the difference in the crime rate between her complex and the surrounding area, she made the courageous choice to hold the landlord accountable. She knew if she did nothing, one of her neighbors would be next, and she took action to stop what happened to her from happening to anyone else. Ottie knew suing the apartment complex owners was the only way to make them change.

Mediation

We'd been litigating the case for almost four years when the apartment complex lawyers reached out to us and asked if we'd be interested in mediation. Trials are expensive and emotional, and they further draw out the process of seeing justice done. Ottie was eighty-two by then, so we agreed to sit down with them.

Mediation (also called "alternative dispute resolution" or ADR) offers a chance for the two sides to avoid a trial and reach an agreement more quickly and with less expense. The mediator is usually a retired judge whose payment isn't linked to the outcome and who isn't personally invested in the case. They serve as a go-between to see if it's possible to broker a resolution everyone can agree to.

Mediation sessions begin with everyone in the same room to briefly introduce the case to the mediator. Each side has a few minutes to explain their position before going into separate conference rooms where they meet privately with the mediator. The mediator then walks between rooms carrying each side's offer to the other and making recommendations based on private conversations with each set of lawyers and her experience as a judge.

Our mediation date had been set months in advance, but as it turned out, our session ended up falling just a few days after my father's funeral. I could have rescheduled, but I didn't want to ask Ottie to wait any longer. I was too keenly aware that time is particularly precious for people in their eighties, and I knew her health wasn't good. The insurance company lawyers knew this too, but it meant something entirely different for them. The lawyer who spoke on behalf of the insurance company was a young man, dressed in expensive clothes, and in great physical shape. He was relaxed, sitting back in his chair and smiling.

"Look," he said. "Let's put aside for the moment whether or not the complex had proper security. Let's assume we're responsible. What are we responsible for? An eighty-one-year-old man lost his life. Which was what—maybe three or four more years? He had cancer. He was almost blind. And Mrs. Lewis suffered some internal injuries, but she's clearly recovered. You want us to pay for the damage, but how much damage was actually done?"

I turned to the mediator and said, "I'm not going to talk to this man. If he puts so little value on the dignity of a family matriarch, I don't think he's worth my client's time."

The insurance lawyer started to argue, but I wasn't done. "The time Joe had left was more valuable because there was less of it. I just spent the last few hours and days of my father's life with him, and I'd pay anything for more time together. That time— the time to say good-bye, to say, 'I love you' and 'thank you' is time Joe's wife and children and grandchildren didn't get. If this young man doesn't recognize the value of that, I'm not going to waste our time trying to convince him."

Ottie and Joe had more in common with my father than their age. They were all people of tremendous character who stayed actively involved in the lives of an entire community well past the age where most people start taking it easy. I wasn't going to let the insurance company lawyer treat them like just another crime statistic. Character counts. My dad had it. Ottie and Joe had it. The insurance company's lawyer did not.

I wrote down a dollar figure. "That is the number," I told the mediator. "They're either going to pay it, or we're going to see them in court."

The amount I'd written down was high (and a record for that kind of case), but I was confident a jury would feel, as I did, that the apartment complex's insurance company didn't have the right to discount an older person's life or a family's grief the way its lawyer was trying to do. And I think he knew I was right.

Insurance

The basic business model for insurance companies is simple. There's not that much difference in how it works for an individual driver and an apartment complex. The insurance company charges a recurring premium in exchange for a promise to cover losses that might occur up to a certain dollar amount. The insurance company spreads the risk of that possibility out over a large group of people. It then decides what to charge the insured party by calculating how likely it is that they'll have to do the thing everyone's paying them to do—cover a loss. The difference between what they charge customers and what they pay on claims is their profit. If the apartment complex had a policy covering them up to X dollars, every dollar less than X that the insurance company paid Ottie was kept from her pocket and stayed in theirs. Of course, they could pay the full policy amount and still be profitable. Insurance companies are very careful to make sure the premiums-in to payments-out balance works in their favor.

Occasionally, insurance companies do the right thing, but if they always acted the way they should, the world wouldn't need lawyers like me. Sadly, they rarely do, and the larger the amount they owe, the more likely they are to take the less honorable path of the three Ds.

THE THREE DS: DENY, DELAY, DEFEND

Deny

Imagine an insurance company whose extensive research and sophisticated prediction models tell them to expect $80,000,000 in claims they'll have to pay. They price their premiums to bring in $100,000,000 in premiums. A truly ethical company would content itself with that $20,000,000 in annual profits (that's $20,000,000 *before* they start investing and earning interest on the $100,000,000 they take in). Unfortunately, that's not what happens. To keep our numbers simple, let's imagine that the $80,000,000 in losses they're expecting conveniently arrives in the form of eighty insured people each at fault for $1,000,000 worth of damages.

If the insurance company can get just one of those cases dropped, they've made an extra $1,000,000, so they just deny it. They'll say it isn't legitimate, or they'll paint a picture of the long, painful, and expensive process they'll make the injured person endure hoping they'll just drop the whole thing.

Delay

If a person doesn't accept their denial, the insurance company will make sure the process takes as long as possible because every day they delay, they get to hold onto the $1,000,000 they owe. And every day it's earning them interest. Delaying things also makes it more likely that the injured person will quit early, agreeing to take some lesser sum. If the insurance company can get even half of the people to take half of what they're owed, they've made another $20,000,000, doubling their profits.

Defend

Finally, if denying and delaying doesn't work, the insurance company will defend the case in court. Of course, this is their right, but even here, they're often less than honest. When the lawyer sitting across the conference table from Ottie introduced himself, he claimed to represent Mr. Smith, the apartment complex owner. That makes it sound like he's working for Mr. Smith, but that isn't who pays his salary. Mr. Smith's insurance company was, and as the old saying goes, "He who pays the fiddler calls the tune."

Mr. Smith might very well have felt terrible about what happened to Ottie and Joe and wanted them to get the total dollar amount of the policy he'd paid for, but it wasn't up to him. I've seen cases in which the insurance company refused to pay the full amount of the policy a "Mr. Smith" held, knowing that a jury verdict above the policy amount left him responsible for the difference. I had to write the CEO of the insurance company a very strongly worded letter reminding him he had a legal responsibility to protect Mr. Smith from personal exposure. It was precisely this protection he'd been buying when he paid his monthly premiums.

Character Counts

When I said the apartment complex's insurance company would either pay the full amount of their policy or see us in court, the lawyer was confused. But the mediator understood, and so did Ottie. The insurance company had hired a lawyer who was not a man of character. He'd made no attempt to hide that fact in front of the mediator, and he wouldn't be able to conceal it from a jury. Of course, many defense lawyers have character, and insurance companies are entitled to a defense, but I won't negotiate with a person who doesn't acknowledge the value of an elderly person's remaining years, a matriarch's dignity, and an entire extended family's grief.

Ottie put her hand on my elbow. She was talking to me, but everyone in the room heard her. "I don't care about the money," she said. "I don't care if I die before they pay. You make them pay for what they did." The mediation was over. We walked out.

Five days later, the mediator called me. The young insurance company lawyer had apparently reported what happened at the mediation and gotten instructions to pay exactly what we'd told them we would accept. The company must have realized a jury wouldn't let them get away with any less. They paid the entire amount, and Ottie lived to see it in an apartment where the security lights were always on, and every building had its own security guard.

Sadly, though, the elderly aren't the only people whose lives and value insurance companies try to minimize. In the next chapter, I'll introduce you to a trucking company that believed a man's life was worthless because he didn't have a place to live.

CHAPTER 2

Prevent the Predictable

David was born in a small manufacturing city in New Jersey. He was the third child, a late surprise whom everyone in the family cherished, but none more than his sister. Ruby was more than happy to give up her spot as the youngest child in the family and was fiercely protective of her brother. Not that David needed protection. He was the star of his high school basketball team and an excellent student. He missed Ruby when she left for college, but he bragged about her to everyone—the first member of his family to get a degree.

David didn't follow in his sister's footsteps. He'd fallen in love with a girl a year younger than he was and didn't want to leave town. He got work as a janitor at the local manufacturing company because jobs on the line were hard to come by. His hard work and contagious cheerfulness quickly caught his supervisor's eye. After a year, right as his girlfriend graduated from high school, David got a promotion. Meg left for school, but they stayed in touch, and when she came home four years later, they reconnected. The spark was still there, and they married within the year.

They wanted kids one day but put it off to simply enjoy each other's company for a while and build up their nest egg. Meg was a bookkeeper, David worked the day shift on the manufacturing line, and together they lived their version of the American dream for ten years. They bought a house and spent their weekends and vacations hiking and camping. Then David lost his job—one of the hundreds laid off when the company moved its manufacturing offshore.

David and Meg had some savings, and they were thinking seriously about starting their own business when Meg got sick. She was diagnosed with stage four breast cancer. For a year and a half, David did everything he could for her. They burned through their savings. Meg fought it hard, but the cancer was aggressive. Finally, after watching his wife suffer immensely, David lost her.

David didn't know what to do with his grief. Out of money and out of work, he self-medicated with alcohol and then drugs. When he lost the house he and Meg had bought, David lived in his car, then on the streets where he lost contact with his family and reality. Eventually, he hit rock bottom and showed up at his sister's house in Newark. Ruby had gone from college to business school. Now, with an MBA and moving quickly toward an executive job, she'd been looking for David. She was relieved to find him alive but heartbroken by his condition and invited him to come live with her. David was too proud. All he wanted was her help in getting sober.

Ruby found a nearby support group for David. After a few months, they started having dinner together once a week. Nine months into his recovery, clean and sober, David asked for Ruby's help finding a job. She did an online search and found a job fair at the local armory. David was nervous, but he was also committed to putting his life back together. He woke up early the morning of the job fair and was walking to the armory when the tire of a poorly maintained passing truck flew off and hit him in the head.

David was rushed to the hospital, where a team of doctors fought to save his life. Ruby stayed with him for days but eventually, the doctors determined David was brain dead. Ruby struggled with the decision and finally signed off on removing him from life support to give his organs a better chance at transplantation. She couldn't believe her baby brother was never going to get the new life he'd worked so hard to get sober for.

Ruby was devastated.

She was also furious. How dare a trucking company put deadly weapons on the road? She simply didn't understand how something like that could be allowed to happen. How does a tire just fly off?

As she struggled to make sense of the tragedy, she learned that the trucking company had chosen not to inspect its trucks, although there were regulations in place that required them to do so. Worse, she found out that across the nation, tires fly off trucks at lethal speeds five hundred times every day. She felt like she had to do something. She wanted to punish the trucking company and put all the ones like it on notice.

She talked to a friend on the police force who told her that the company hadn't followed regulations and later falsified their records, but neither of those things was a crime. There was nothing for the police to do. Ruby didn't understand. Her brother had been killed. The trucking company could have kept it from happening. Why wasn't anyone going to jail? Were there really no legal consequences for killing pedestrians with flying tires?

There aren't.

Ruby's friend told her the only way to keep the same thing from happening again was to sue, but he urged her to let go of her outrage. There wasn't anything she could do, and she didn't need the money. Even if she sued, he told her, David would just be some homeless guy to the insurance company. His death wouldn't cost them enough to change their practices or deter other companies from being equally careless. Ruby didn't care. Even when David lost everything, he had never given up. Neither would she.

When she came to see me, I had to tell Ruby that her friends were right. The trucking company hadn't done anything illegal, and the insurance company would argue that homeless and unemployed, David's life wasn't worth much.

I also told her she was right. The trucking company *shouldn't* get to decide it was okay for them to do what they'd done, and I thought a jury would agree. In America, we, the people, determine what is and isn't acceptable behavior for companies that do business in our communities.

Juries

When I start preparing to take a case to trial, I write down the last thing I will say first. A lawyer's summation is what we get to tell jury members just before they go into a private room alone to make their decision. I build everything I plan to say throughout the trial to lead up to that moment and land on target with maximum impact. That target is an idea—the theme or key point that I want the jury to consider as they make their final decisions.

At the heart of every case is the violation of a simple moral rule—one my client had trusted would be followed only to have that trust betrayed. In David and Ruby's story, the rule-breaking was obvious; the company had chosen cheap and easy over safe and responsible. They didn't inspect their trucks properly. They falsified records. They ignored warning signs because they didn't care as much about the danger they were putting pedestrians in as they cared about saving a few bucks and even fewer minutes. All too often, wrongful death cases involve violating the moral rule of putting people before profits. It's a rule that I believe we have a duty to ask juries to uphold and enforce.

People sometimes think jurors base their decisions about where to place blame and how much companies should pay on the facts of a case, but they don't. People weigh the evidence and follow the logic, but they make up their minds in their hearts. They don't come to a rational decision; they make a moral and emotional judgment. And that's the way it should be.

This is the reason we don't have professional juries. In our legal system, the people who ultimately decide whether or not to teach trucking companies not to kill people with tires are members of our community. They're teachers, waiters, and accountants—ordinary people because it's a jury's job to be the voice of its community and tell the companies what is and is not okay. Juries determine what standards businesses are expected to follow. It's an enormous amount of power, and it comes with an equal weight of responsibility.

In David's case, the jury would consider the fundamental moral question at its heart: what do we value most, people or profits? Are companies that put trucks on our community's roads required to ensure those trucks are safe—at least safe enough not to launch 105-pound tires at lethal speeds where people are walking? Had the company inspected their trucks as required, David would be alive, and we wouldn't be taking them to court.

Instead, they'd done nothing to make sure their trucks were safe. They'd ignored warning signs, neglected inspections, falsified documents, and decided regulations didn't apply to them. Now, they asked the jury to say it was okay—to reward them for not doing their job.

A jury's verdict is the voice of a community's conscience. It speaks volumes about what that community values and creates a lasting record of its moral judgment. It also shapes the future because actions that are rewarded are repeated. It's a heavy responsibility to put on ordinary people. Still, over and over, I've seen juries rise to the challenge and hold companies accountable. I've learned to have great faith in our jury system. It no longer surprises—but will always inspire—me.

Closure

A jury's verdict is a message to both sides—the plaintiff (that's us) and the defendant (the trucking company). To the jury, it would be a moral statement. For Ruby, it would be an emotional one. Concluding her case against the trucking company would mark the end of what can be a long and is inevitably a painful process. I warned Ruby about this. As I always tell people considering a wrongful death suit, I told Ruby that sometimes it's better to simply walk away and let the emotional wounds start to heal. Particularly when the person killed was young, those left grieving their loss are also dealing with a great deal of shock. They can't really believe what's happened. They never imagined being in a situation like this. Often, they're not even sure what they're doing in a lawyer's office. They know nothing the courts can do will bring their loved one back. But from the moment I met Ruby, I could tell she had the emotional strength to see the process through.

Being involved in litigation is emotionally taxing. Sometimes, the best thing for a family is to put as much of the tragedy behind them as possible. Of course, they never forget the person they lost, and the pain of it never completely goes away, but it does fade. Years after their daughter's death, Jenny's parents still cried when they talked to my dad on the fairgrounds.

But I also saw them laughing with other kids in the popcorn line, and their joy and pride were obvious on their faces when that year's scholarship recipient thanked them. As I've said, every one of my cases has, at its heart, a betrayal of trust and a violation of a moral law. Where there has been a wrong, closure—making it right and moving on—is achieved in two ways: either punishment or repentance and forgiveness.

Repentance and Forgiveness

Repentance is a three-step process. The first step is acknowledgment. Acknowledgment is the opposite of denial and means that we acknowledge what we did was wrong. We don't pretend it never happened or that it wasn't our fault. We accept our responsibility.

The second step is apology. We admit we did something wrong and that bad things happened to someone as a result, and we say we are sorry.

The final step of true repentance is to make things right. We must provide restitution for the harms and damages caused by our actions. There is no true repentance without this step. Without restitution, there are only empty apologies.

The trucking company couldn't even get past the first step. They refused to acknowledge any responsibility, insisting they'd done nothing wrong. Ruby deserved closure, and although a jury couldn't force the trucking company to apologize, it could tell them they were wrong and force them to provide full restitution.

In the end, that's exactly what the jury did.

As a society, we've agreed that we no longer want to pursue "eye-for-an-eye" justice. We didn't ask a jury to order the execution of the trucking company's president. Instead, we asked them to tell the company (and others like it) that David's life had value using the same measurement we use for the value of a worker's time or to say what a car is worth—money. The substantial verdict it returned didn't bring David back, and it didn't make his death "worth it." It did motivate the trucking company to change the way it inspected tires. And it brought Ruby closure. She took a stand, and a jury honored his memory, bringing her some closure on the entire event.

SIDEBAR

Wrongful death and catastrophic injury payments are never taxed because the law recognizes they're not gains or profits. As restitution, they're intended, to the limited extent it's possible, to make the injured "whole" for the loss they suffered. It's this "making whole" that brings people closure.

When we first talked, I understood that this was what Ruby was looking for, but I warned her it would take years. So soon after David's terrible death, her mind was still full of the agonizing decision she'd had to make to take him off of life support. The image of him walking to the job fair in his new second-hand suit, nervous and hopeful when the tire flew off the truck and killed him, haunted her. Over time, she'd be able to focus more on the happy memories she had of their childhood together and on the great life David had had with Meg, but every time someone from my office called Ruby, David's death would come back to her. The litigation would keep the pain fresh.

Ruby understood, but she was determined. The lawsuit would keep David present in the trucking company's mind too. It infuriated her to think that otherwise, it wouldn't give David's life or death another thought. Why should this company be able to go on about its business, disregarding other people's safety while she was left with all this grief and rage? "Besides," she told me, "it's the right thing to do. If another tire from one of their trucks kills someone else and I hadn't tried everything to stop it, I'd never forgive myself. Plenty of people walked along that road every day."

I agreed. I told Ruby that I consider advocating for potential future victims to be part of my job. I'm a deterrence lawyer. If Ruby was willing to put herself through the process of holding that trucking company accountable, I stood ready to do everything I could to help.

We went to work, did the due diligence, and found the company had been previously cited for the same and other safety violations. They really were a hazard to the community. David's death had been preventable—even predictable. If a company doesn't maintain its trucks' axles, tires will predictably do exactly what the one that killed David did—hurl one hundred-plus pounds of steel-reinforced rubber into the air. It's a known issue. It's why federal regulations mandate that companies inspect their axles once a year. It doesn't take a lot of time or cost much money, but this company opted not to bother and forged its documentation.

Predictable and Preventable

David's death was not an accident. Accidents are unforeseeable and, as a result, not something you can protect yourself or others against. The trucking company certainly didn't intend to kill anyone (that would be murder), but they didn't intend *not* to. That's what prevention is. It's what you do—or in this case, fail to do—when you intend not to let people be killed by things you can predict will happen. Had the company valued safety and wanted to keep flying tires from killing someone, they would have taken action to prevent it, just as federal regulations require them to.

Companies have a responsibility to prevent what's predictable. When they don't, juries' money verdicts are the American legal system's method of justice.

The trucking company's insurance tried to avoid paying what it owed by suggesting David's life wasn't worth much because he was jobless and homeless. The jury thought otherwise. Their verdict taught the trucking company it couldn't shirk responsibility without paying a heavy price for disregarding other people's safety.

But trying to diminish the worth of a lost life isn't the only way insurance companies dodge their obligations. Often, when they know they can't get away with paying less, they suggest an ulterior motive.

CHAPTER 3

It's Never About the Money

Lily was almost five when she was killed.

It was cold on the day she died. She had been playing across the street at her friend's house and decided to run home to get her purple mittens so she and her friend could play outside.

Lily's mom got the purple mittens from the box in the closet where they'd been tucked away all summer and a not-purple hat for good measure. Lily didn't want the hat at first, but her brother and grandad were in the yard with their hats on, so Lily decided she would wear hers too.

With her hat and mittens, Lily was already running when her mom followed her outside to call, "Do you want boots?" from the porch. Her brother screamed her name. It was the last thing Lily heard.

Sam didn't hear anything from where he sat in the appliance repair van. He just felt the impact of Lily's small body. Then everyone came running. Later, he would testify he'd been trying to read a street number on the opposite side of the road.

When he ran over Lily, he was looking forward again, but the GPS unit above the front left dash blocked his view out of the windshield.

Sam worked for a national home repair and renovation company that offered a discount to customers if its technicians didn't get to their houses within the two-hour window its schedulers provided. The company put GPS devices in their trucks to track their drivers and feed them the fastest route between house visits. Sam was driving under time pressure and with an obstructed view when he hit Lily. His company blamed Lily's mom.

Motive and Fault

Questions about why people and companies took (or failed to take) certain actions are often at the core of wrongful death and catastrophic injury cases, and they can be difficult to answer. It's a fairly straightforward matter to establish the facts of what happened, but juries don't make decisions based on the facts. When they're asked to decide who was at fault for a life-ending or altering outcome, juries are much more interested in questions of *why*.

That's why the themes I build my cases around often speak to motive. For example, in the last chapter, I said the trucking company ignored regulations, skipped safety procedures, and falsified documents because it valued profits more than people. It's hard to see another reason for their actions. Even their insurance company's lawyers couldn't offer much of an alternative explanation beyond trying to suggest the outcome was an accident. In other words, killing people *wasn't* the motive. I believe this is why they tried to convince the jury that David's life wasn't worth much.

The legal terms for this split between why something happened and how much value was lost as a result are *fault* (or *liability*) and *damage*. In Lily's case, the insurance lawyer tried to make motive an issue in both. They blamed Lily's mother for her child's death and claimed Lily's brother (who was eighteen by the time we got to trial) was motivated by greed.

Respondeat Superior

The *respondeat superior* doctrine is designed to prevent the kind of chaos that would result if businesses had no incentive to hire qualified people or to train and supervise them. By holding employers legally responsible for their employees' actions (or inactions) while they're at work, the law gives companies a financial reason to prevent their employees from hurting themselves or others.

The doctrine of *respondeat superior* makes a company legally responsible no matter what, but rarely is that fact the sole reason for its responsibility when a tragedy occurs. Usually, it runs deeper and into motive. The thing that often motivates a company to be lax in its oversight of employees and disregard common-sense safety procedures is greed. The company cuts corners or puts unsafe practices in place to either save money or make more money. As I remember Dad pointing out to me on the ride home from the carnival, the driver of the bus that killed Jennifer was in danger of having his pay docked by the city. The trucking company that killed David falsified records to keep its trucks on the road without any downtime. Sam was driving under time pressure and with reduced visibility because his company had implemented policies and installed devices that served it, not him, and killed Lily. So rather than accept responsibility, apologize, and make things right, they chose to try and blame her mother.

Polarization

When the insurance company and their lawyers refuse to acknowledge how their actions contributed to the event that led to the tragedy, I will often highlight that for the jury by polarizing the case.[3] With Lily's death, there was only one question with one of two answers which polarized the case. Either the family was lying to cheat the company, or the company was lying to cheat the family. The defense lawyers claimed that Lily was run over because she wasn't adequately supervised. Never mind that her mother was on the stoop and her brother and granddad in the yard. Put aside the rural cul-de-sac that displayed large "Children at Play" signs and was more like a driveway than a road. Ignore that it was a Saturday when not even a school bus was expected to be on the remote cul-de-sac. Either her mom was negligent for not escorting Lily to and from the neighbor's house, holding her hand and thus at fault for Lily's death, or the company with a policy that caused their drivers to speed between appointments with a large, view-obstructing GPS device in the lower left windshield of a two-ton truck was.

This was a frivolous defense. It was absurd and cruel, and I don't believe even the lawyers making it believed it. Maybe they were hoping to use it as an excuse to dig up every unkind

3 *Polarizing the Case: Exposing and Defeating the Malingering Myth*, by Rick Friedman is a highly recommended book for all trial lawyers.

or embarrassing thing they could find about the mother to lower the amount the jury awarded in damages. Maybe it was just a delay tactic, and they planned to change their position after we'd done all the work to prepare for trial. Maybe they just thought it was their only chance to get out of paying, so they might as well give it a shot. When people use the word "frivolous" to describe a lawsuit or its defense, it's exactly this exaggerated disconnect from good sense and morality they're referring to.

Frivolous Court Cases

Of course, you hear a lot more about frivolous suits than you do about frivolous defenses like the one in this case because defense lawyers pump a great deal of money into the conversation. They take out ads and influence politicians. They claim they're trying to protect ordinary citizens from the high insurance premiums that companies are forced to pay and pass on to consumers. They're really working for the large companies they represent. They're also ignoring that insurance companies would be able (in fact forced) to lower premiums if companies behaved ethically and didn't force claims to be filed by refusing to accept responsibility when their insured kill or seriously injure people.

The defense attorneys' biggest triumph in the war for public opinion was the famous McDonald's coffee case. In a moment, I'll explain the dishonesty of their argument, but first, consider the larger context. Defense attorney organizations are fighting to convince the public that frivolous lawsuits are a big problem. They're spending a lot on this battle, even though they have no real opponent. They're fighting to close the doors of the courtroom for these individual claims. The threat of the power ordinary people have to sue companies that kill or seriously injure them may be the only thing making our world relatively safe from reckless drivers or cars that explode.

MCDONALD'S COFFEE

The story, as the defense spun it, and as it reached the popular imagination, goes something like this: Some greedy idiot buys a cup of coffee at McDonald's and is drinking it in her car. She's using her thighs as a cupholder but forgets and squeezes her legs together, forcing the coffee out of its cup and onto her legs, causing a mild burn. She sues for millions and wins. She must have been crazy. Her lawyer must have been crazy. The jury must have been crazy too, and the jury system can't be trusted.

It's a story that benefits corporations. It puts all the focus on the injured party, suggesting they did it to themselves and that the company is blameless. And the media, which get their advertising revenue from those corporations, have no incentive to challenge that narrative.

In court, however, you have to prove what you say with evidence supported by facts. Here are the facts: The seventy-nine-year-old woman, Stella Liebeck, took complete responsibility for the spill. She just thought that if McDonald's hadn't served its coffee at temperatures very close to boiling, she wouldn't have suffered third-degree burns which required multiple skin grafts, eight days in the hospital, and two subsequent years of medical interventions. She asked McDonald's for the cost of her treatment—$20,000. She asked them only to cover treatment she wouldn't have needed had she spilled properly heated coffee that would not have caused the severe burns she suffered.

McDonald's offered her $800. Stella sued them for what she'd had to pay out of her own pocket, nothing extra.

After listening to the story in much more depth than I've related here and having heard McDonald's acknowledge that they intentionally served coffee that was too hot for consumption and hazardous if spilled (they'd already had hundreds of burns reported), the jury decided the multinational company should pay Stella close to three million dollars over the cost of her medical bills.[4] That's just one day of coffee sales for McDonald's, but it sent the message that what they'd done was not acceptable. Following the jury's verdict, McDonald's changed the way it heats and serves coffee.

That's what happened. But McDonald's had a multimillion-dollar PR budget, and Stella Liebeck didn't, so we, the public, heard only the version they spun. We heard it was a frivolous lawsuit. It wasn't. Stella Liebeck had the courage, with her lawyer, to take on one of the largest companies in the world and held them accountable for prioritizing profits over the safety of their customers.

Just like McDonald's tried to blame the person they injured, the national home repair and renovation company that prioritized speed over safety tried to blame Lily's mom for her daughter's death. Such frivolous defenses only stop when jurors, like the McDonald's jury, vote for a substantial verdict. Rest assured, the national home repair and renovation company won't be so quick to blame the people they hurt, given the outcome of Lily's case.

4 McDonald's wanted to increase their coffee sales and performed studies on how to best get people to buy coffee on the way to work. McDonald's learned if they served their coffee near boiling, the coffee would still be hot by the time the customer got to work. Even though McDonald's knew heating the coffee to such extreme temperatures was dangerous and would cause significant burns if it was spilled, they chose to do it anyway because sales were more important than safety.

Guilt

Every parent I've met who has suffered through the death of a child carries with them a weight of guilt in addition to their grief, whether the death was the result of natural causes or not. Lily's mom, Annabelle, was no exception, and I knew the other side would try to take advantage of it. This never fails to make me angry. Annabelle had already been through so much, and it wasn't her fault. But mothers can't help but blame themselves, and big companies are all too happy to use decent people's overdeveloped sense of responsibility to dodge their own.

Before a case goes to trial, there is a process called *discovery*, during which both sides discover all relevant information about the case from the other side. As a part of that process, lawyers always get depositions (answers to questions given under oath) from anyone involved. As I prepared Annabelle for her deposition, we often talked about her feelings, and guilt rose right to the top. She remembered how many shades and styles of purple she'd seen at Lily's funeral. The little girl had been known and loved by people in the neighborhood, at school, in peewee sports, and their church community. All of these people also knew Annabelle as an attentive and involved mom. Rationally, Annabelle knew Lily's death wasn't her fault. Still, on some deep emotional level, she believed a mother's job was to protect her babies, and she hadn't been able to protect her Lily.

As we talked through her feelings and her stories of Lily's birthdays and hobbies, their family camping trips, and holidays, Annabelle gradually began to see her mothering wasn't defined by the one terrible moment of Lily's death. She'd been a wonderful, involved, and loving mother, and nobody had any right to say otherwise. I encouraged her to see the intensity of her grief for what it was—a function of the strength of her love, not an indication of guilt. I also affirmed her right to be angry. The corporate lawyer had chosen to blame Annabelle and suggest she was not an attentive mom, which I knew was outrageous. We were pursuing a wrongful death action because Lily's death was wrongful, and the party responsible was refusing to accept any accountability.

I was deeply offended on her behalf by the other side's suggestion, but she needed to be prepared for them to try to make her feel at fault. The insurance company had no shame and would try to shrug off their responsibility and dump it on her. Annabelle would probably always be haunted by "what ifs" centered on the company's choice to obstruct the view of their drivers, but she was able to get absolutely clear that their choices caused Lily's death.

During Annabelle's deposition, when the lawyers began asking questions that implied Lily hadn't been adequately supervised, she let out a roar I heard two floors away. Annabelle channeled all her grief and outrage into it and shut that line of questioning down. She'd gotten angry—angry that the service company had allowed an unsafe truck to drive down the street where children played, angry that they'd put their drivers under time pressure that made them feel rushed, and angry that they were trying to shift the blame for the results of their carelessness and callousness onto her.

Not every client I work with achieves the kind of clarity Annabelle did, but it's a dynamic I see play out in almost every case. A company blames the people it hurts and adds guilt to their grief. The machinery of corporate America does this preemptively, pushing the myth of frivolous lawsuits so effectively that many potential clients show up in my office feeling guilty for even considering a suit against a company that has shown no remorse for what it did to them.

I suspect Annabelle's powerful response during her deposition contributed to the insurance company's change of tactics, but they may have planned it from the outset. Either way, the day before the trial began, they decided not to fight the liability (fault) portion of the case. For us, ironically, this was almost a worst-case scenario. We'd spent thousands of dollars establishing the facts of what happened. We'd deposed Sam and knew he had never even seen Lily. He hadn't hit his horn, used his brakes, or tried to swerve. We had photographs of the GPS mounted on the dash of his truck blocking the corner of window where she would have been visible. It was a position that violated both federal statutes and company policy. We'd commissioned an animated video of what happened and documented the dent on the left front bumper. But no longer needing the work we'd done wasn't the reason I was disappointed in this last-minute change of tactics.

By accepting liability, the defense thought they would prevent us from telling the jury exactly what they did to cause Lily's death. They did not want a jury to hear how they intentionally violated federal rules prohibiting the placement of GPS devices in front of the windshield on commercial vehicles, how they emphasized speed instead of safety with their drivers, and how they were blaming Annabelle for her own daughter's death.

However, their decision to accept responsibility did not eliminate our ability to tell a jury what they'd done. I'd conducted focus groups and was confident the defense's strategy of blaming Annabelle would anger jury members as much as it angered me. By accepting liability (fault), they tried not to risk offending the jury's sense of justice (in much the way McDonald's had), recognizing that an angry jury is likely to deliver larger settlements.

In this instance, however, the insurance company had added to the damage done to Lily's family by trying to blame Annabelle when they knew she'd done nothing wrong. For more than two years, she'd had to prepare to defend herself against their accusations, and it had taken an enormous toll on her psychologically. The fact that they were finally taking responsibility didn't erase the damage they had inflicted on Annabelle through their defense tactics, and it didn't keep me from revealing their calculating and cruel strategy to the people on the jury. A world-renowned psychiatrist examined Annabelle and determined the defense tactics of blaming her worsened her grief. Through the doctor's expert testimony, I was able to show the jury the additional damage the company had done by blaming Annabelle for the tragedy it now admitted wasn't her fault.

Motive and Damages

When a company accepts responsibility, the liability portion of our suit against them no longer gets tried. Rather than asking the jury to determine where the fault lies, we're asking them only to determine who was injured and the extent of the harm caused as a consequence. In Chapter 9, I'll go into more detail about the factors we ask juries to consider in making this determination. Here, I want to discuss how the insurance company, having given up on making Lily's mom look responsible, tried to instead paint her grieving family as in it for the money.

In wrongful death and catastrophic injury cases, my clients—the people harmed by a company's betrayal of common-sense safety principles—are called the plaintiffs. In almost every case, the insurance company tries to put a negative stain on their motives. They usually do this by implying my clients are simply greedy, even though this is never the case.

In wrongful death cases, it's never about the money.

Most often, the plaintiffs in wrongful death cases act to keep what happened to their loved one from happening to anyone else. Their motivation is to protect others. This was certainly what motivated both Jennifer's parents and Lily's. A sense of responsibility to the person who was killed or the need to honor their memory can add to someone's reasons for putting themselves through the pain of pursuing a wrongful death case.

An insurance company can't understand (or won't acknowledge) these motivations. To it, everything is about money. Just like the thief who constantly expects to be robbed, insurance companies act as if everyone—even a grieving mother—is motivated by the things that drive them—money and greed. But here's a little thought experiment for you: Do you think one member of the jury would have voluntarily had water hot enough to require multiple skin grafts poured over their thighs and genitals for $2.9 million? Would anyone accept any amount of money to watch their child be run over by a truck? Money damages represent our society's advancement from a time when "eye for an eye" damages were considered appropriate. We no longer inflict the same harm on the wrongdoer but seek to make the person who was damaged whole. While money never truly makes anyone "whole," it is the best option we have.

I've delivered millions and millions of dollars to people, and the bigger the check, the faster they say, "I would give it all back to have none of this ever happen in the first place." Every last one of my clients would give every penny back to return to the life they had the day before the event that caused their tragedy. Only one client in thirty-two years of practice has ever told me the settlement made their suffering worthwhile. (I'll tell you his story in Chapter 9.) With catastrophic injury or wrongful death cases, greed never has anything to do with why people sue.

Greed motivated the service company to install a GPS unit where it blocked Sam's view of the street and to keep its drivers under constant time pressure. Greed motivated the insurance company to try and shift responsibility from the service company to Annabelle. And when that frivolous defense failed, it accused the family of greed. "Money wouldn't bring Lily back," they'd point out. All a large verdict would do was make the family rich.

The insurance company chose Lily's brother Franco to target for this scurrilous argument. He'd been just eight when Lily was killed and had struggled with a terrible sense of guilt since witnessing her death. He'd started lifting weights in high school, and when he took the stand at seventeen, he was so muscular he barely fit in his suit. He couldn't quite forgive himself for having not saved his sister, and he looked like a man who planned never to feel helpless again. The lawyer for the other side approached him smiling. "A young man like you, I'm sure you have all kinds of things you could do with a financial windfall, right?" he said with a chuckle.

But it wasn't funny to Franco. "I owe it to Lily to stand up to you," he said. "She used to count our grapes at lunch to make sure we both had the same. She used to mix up her socks—one purple, one blue—because blue was her friend's favorite color.

She got really mad when anything was unfair. If she died and nothing changed, if nothing good came out of it, she'd never forgive us. They took away my sister. There must be consequences for their actions. Otherwise, this will likely happen again. My parents and I talked long and hard about coming to trial, and after a lot of reflection, even though we knew it would be hard, we knew we had to do it—not just for Lily but for our neighbors too. We want to make sure this never happens again."

When I questioned Franco, I pointed out to him (and by extension to the jury), what the other side was trying to suggest—that nine years after Lily's death, Franco was a senior in college, he'd already moved on. I wanted to give him a chance to address what they'd implied directly, so I asked him, "Have you moved on?"

"The shock of that day has passed, but the pain has not. Sure, I've kept living," he said. "But Lily is with me every day."

"What keeps her so present in your mind?" I asked him.

"I got a tattoo."

"What tattoo did you get?"

The tough, heavily muscled young man took a deep breath. "A purple bunny."

"Why a purple bunny?"

"Lily had this little stuffed toy rabbit she called Bunbun. She carried it everywhere, and it was falling apart. I mean just half an ear, eye hanging by a thread. She was going to give it up for her fifth birthday. She said she would be too big for it then, but…"

"Did you keep it?" I asked.

"Bunbun? No." Franco swallowed hard. "I thought about it, but I gave it back. Bunbun's with Lily in case…"

Franco needed a moment, and frankly, so did I.

Franco cleared his throat. "Bunbun is with Lily, but Lily is with me," he said. "And so is her goofy rabbit. It's on my arm."

"Can you show the jury?" I asked him.

"That'd be a little tricky because I'm wearing a jacket and tie and a long sleeve shirt," he said. "And Bunbun's now a tattoo up high on the inside of my left arm."

"Where no one can see it?" I asked.

"I don't need anyone to see it," Franco said. "I have it on the inside of my arm because it is closest to my heart."

I had no further questions. Franco stepped off the witness stand, and there was total silence in the courtroom. Afterward, Franco told me he didn't care what the jury did because he knew he'd done what he had to. He'd stood up for Lily and told her story. Testifying helped bring him a level of closure he hadn't realized he needed.

Blame and Hope

When a family buries a child, it often feels like hope has gone into the ground as well. Certainly, all of Lily's possibilities were taken away with her life. She never turned five. She never had a high school graduation or a wedding. Her parents' hopes for their daughter died with her, but other hopes endure, and new hopes begin.

For the first few years after Lily's death, grief replaced almost everything in her family's life. Her birthday and Christmas are still tinged with it. I am sure they always will be. To my mind, any family that survives such a loss deserves to feel a degree of pride in coping with such heartbreak. And to every family I meet in the middle of a hope-stripped wasteland, I can only offer the perspective of time and experience. To some, I can offer a legal process for putting the blame where it belongs.

I wore a purple tie to the last day of Lily's trial. In my summation, I reminded the jury of Franco's tattoo. He wore Lily's bunny rabbit as a symbolic reminder of what his sister had meant and the obligation her death created for him. I told the jury, "That service company is responsible for Lily's death. They're not arguing that. They are, however, suggesting there's nothing they can do about it. The money won't bring Lily back. And they're right. The money won't fix anything. So, ladies and gentlemen, why return a significant verdict as I'm asking you to? For its symbolic value.

"Symbols have enormous power. It's why we wear wedding rings to represent a promise. It's why we stand to show respect when the judge enters this room. Our laws recognize this power and put it in your hands to use. Your verdict will be a symbol of how much value we put on the life of a child and on this child's wrongful death. In twenty years, people will be able to come back to this courtroom and see your verdict. You are the ones empowered to determine what your verdict will stand for. If you believe companies should not violate federal safety statutes preventing GPS units from blocking the drivers view; if you believe companies should not prioritize speed over safety; then your verdict speaks volumes as to how important following these safety rules are in our community.

"The service company placed so little value on Lily's life that it allowed its money-saving GPS units to block a child-sized portion of their trucks' windshields. It had acknowledged it violated safety rules that led to Lily's death but argued the violations weren't that important. I'm asking you to say otherwise because, believe me, other trucking companies are watching. They will learn what you teach them today. Lily's family is asking you to teach them it is not acceptable to violate regulations intended to protect everyone's safety." The jury sent that message clearly, recognizing the company's defense as frivolous, and emphasized their point by demanding record-setting damages for Lily's family.

Money is never the motivation behind my clients' legal action, but it is a powerful symbol and teaching tool. It is also, for better or worse, quite literally the currency of our justice system. It's the mechanism juries have for punishing companies that violate safety regulations and breaking the trust of the communities in which they operate. It's how they teach other companies that they must take reasonable steps to prevent the predictable. It's never about the money, but a money verdict that sends a message can make a difference to grieving families. In the next chapter, you'll meet a family for whom it was particularly important and see why it's so important that justice be accessible to everyone.

CHAPTER 4

Justice Must Be Accessible

Eddie and Jose were having trouble behaving for their grandmother. It was Christmas Eve, and their mom was out doing some last-minute shopping. Their dad was still at work, and the boys were doing their best to behave, but they were too excited to sit still. Martina, their mom, was hurrying to get back to them. She knew they were a lot for her mother to manage, and she wanted to get home in time to take the boys to the park before it got dark. She thought maybe if they wore themselves out, there was a chance they'd fall asleep at a reasonable hour.

Carlos was excited to get home to his wife and boys too. It was going to be the family's best Christmas yet. In the middle of a blistering hot summer, Carlos had taken a job as an apprentice machinist and was making better money than he ever had. He was proud of that and of the skills he was learning operating an industrial lathe.[5] He'd been trained by Paul, a master machinist, and had big plans to make it to that level himself one day.

As Martina got on the bus headed for home, she texted her mother to say she was on her way and asked her to get the boys ready for the park. At the factory, the Christmas party had started, and Paul called to Carlos to come join the fun.

5   An industrial lathe looks like a giant, open-sided six-by-four-foot electric pencil sharpener that "sharpens" metal bars into machine parts by spinning it rapidly against blades.

"I'm just going to finish this job," Carlos called back. He had a dozen of Martina's homemade tamales in his locker to give to Paul. The tamales were Carlos's way of thanking the older man for training him. As he prepared the $90,000 lathe, Carlos replayed Paul's voice in his head.

"You have to be careful here, man. The machine was designed wrong. We have to run it with this part of the metal bar exposed 'cause the safety guards don't work."

"Why haven't they fixed it?" Carlos had asked.

"I don't know. We told the manufacturer they have a problem with the design, but they won't do anything about it."

That Christmas Eve, Carlos set up the machine as he'd been instructed, and it cut off his arm. Without safety guards to keep the metal bar contained, the machine spun it too fast, the bar bent and whipped, hitting Carlos in the shoulder. In an instant, his arm was gone.

Martina was at the park with her boys when she answered a call from her husband's number and heard Paul's voice. She smiled thinking Carlos must have given him the tamales already. But Paul wasn't calling to say thank you. He said, "Carlos got hurt. It's pretty bad. The ambulance was going to Mercy General. I'm sorry. I—"

Emotion choked Paul's words, and it frightened Martina. Chills ran down the back of her neck. "Is it serious?" she asked, already knowing the answer.

Paul responded, "Get to the hospital as fast as you can."

By the time she got to the hospital, Carlos was in surgery. A nurse explained that the doctors were working hard to save his arm, but it would be a long time before they knew anything. Four hours later, when the surgeon came out to speak with her, Martina got the only Christmas present she'd been praying for. "It was touch-and-go there for a while," he told her. "But we were able to reattach the arm. He's strong and healthy. He's got a long road ahead of him, but we think he's going to be okay."

Martina was so relieved she could have hugged the doctor, but she just thanked him, crying, and called home. The boys hadn't eaten much dinner and were extraordinarily well-behaved. They knew something scary had happened to their dad, and they were frightened. On speakerphone, Martina gave them all the good news.

She waited a long time at the hospital, hoping they'd let her see Carlos, but she finally went home, exhausted. She set out the gifts from Santa and fell asleep on the sofa. The hospital called before sunrise on Christmas morning to say Carlos was dead. During the night, he'd gone into cardiac arrest, and while the doctors did all they could to save him, the trauma of his injury was too much for his body to overcome. He had passed away at 4:30 a.m.

When I met Martina a few months later, her boys still didn't trust her when she promised they'd be okay. In their minds, she'd lied about their dad being okay after his work accident. It was making them cagey and withdrawn, and it was breaking her heart. Worse, she confessed, she wasn't sure she could support them on her own. She didn't know if she could earn enough money to keep them in their apartment, and she did not want her boys to worry.

Carlos had worked incredibly hard to rent a place in a good school district. Since the workers' compensation she was getting was just a fraction of what he had earned, Martina was struggling to make rent and worried she'd soon need to disrupt her sons' lives, taking them away from their home, school, and friends. Paul had told her to look into a case against the machine manufacturer because it should have designed a safety guard to cover the metal bar that killed Carlos. She'd come to see me because she was too polite to refuse his suggestion.

Martina knew Carlos had worked a machine designed and manufactured by a huge, multibillion-dollar, international corporation that could drag the case out for years and spend millions on a team of lawyers. Who could she find to go head-to-head with them, much less go dollar-to-dollar on the research, experts, and other spending? She couldn't afford to pay for a consultation. She needed every dollar to keep her kids fed and in school, so before we went any further, she needed to make sure Paul was right, and this visit with me was free. She was afraid she was wasting my time.

I assured her that she wasn't and explained something not many people know—lawyers take injury and wrongful death cases on a contingency basis. That means we don't get paid unless the case is won and then only as a percentage of the final settlement. If the case is lost, no fee is owed to the lawyers. The US legal system is structured this way to ensure everyone, regardless of financial status, can pursue injury claims against wealthy corporations.

Contingent Payment

Justice is built into the foundation of our democracy. No system can be truly democratic if access to justice is restricted only to those able to pay a lawyer's hourly rate (typically between $250 to $750 an hour) for the hundreds of hours it takes to bring a case to trial. Wealthy individuals and corporations who can easily afford it can walk right through the front door of any courthouse in the US. Lawyers who agree to work on a contingency basis enable those who can't afford the hourly rates to enter the courthouse through the figurative "side door." It's how people like Martina gain access to justice. It's the only way a person can take a multibillion-dollar company to court. Lady justice is blind, but only if one can get access to the judicial process. Contingency cases are what keep justice based on merit, not wealth.

Of course, corporations would like to close that pesky side door, and they continuously try to block individuals from accessing the courthouse.

In the previous chapter, I explained why big business likes to suggest it's the victim of frivolous lawsuits and frequently presses for tort[6] reform. But the current system already protects companies by making litigation expensive for lawyers who take on contingency cases. Contingency lawyers advance the cost of experts and spend hundreds of hours on cases with a real risk they may lose that money and never be paid for their time. Every case we take is a risk, and it doesn't always pay off.

Any one of my clients, for any reason, can decide to walk away from a case. If it goes on too long or becomes too emotionally taxing, they can quit and lose nothing and owe nothing. Whatever investments in time and money lawyers have already made on that person's behalf are lost.

6 "Tort" is the legal word for having done the wrong thing (or failing to do the right thing), which ends up hurting someone. "Tort reform" means changing the laws that say how responsible a company is when its actions or inactions harm or kill someone like Carlos.

Beyond that danger, it would be an insane business model for any lawyer to go forward with a frivolous claim. With our time and money invested in preparing a case to go to trial, even if the client remains, the lawyer must go before a judge and prove the case has merit. In other words, before we get a chance to ask for any money, we must establish that our client was harmed by the company we're suing. If we don't—if the case is frivolous—it never sees a courtroom, our clients get nothing, and we lose everything we've invested. No sane lawyer would take a case like Martina's if they didn't believe it had merit based on an expert's opinion.

Many sane lawyers wouldn't take it even if they did have expert support. Her case was particularly risky, not because there was any question of its merit (there wasn't), but because Martina was already under such extraordinary financial pressure. The company that manufactured the machine that killed Carlos wasn't worried about her at all. They were confident she'd never show up or would collapse under the pressure of a trial. Certainly, she'd take less money sooner rather than wait longer for more. For lawyers paid a percentage of the final settlement, a smaller settlement means a lower legal fee, and that alone would have been enough to convince some to stay away.

It didn't scare me. To me, litigating wrongful death cases is more of a public service than an income stream. I don't take on cases I don't believe in deeply enough to be willing to lose the time and money needed to invest in my clients' cause. I also knew something about Carlos that the company lawyers didn't. Everything the man had done, from the apartment he rented to the job he worked, was done to give his children a better life than he'd had. Every year, his family had moved closer to living out the American dream. "If I lost that," Martina told me, "Carlos would never forgive me." She was determined to do whatever it took to make the company provide for her children the way the man it killed would have, and I was willing to invest my firm's money and time to help her see it through.

But Martina was reluctant (as many of my clients initially are) to start a lawsuit. She was worried that Paul, as Carlos's supervisor, might get in trouble, but I explained we wouldn't be suing Paul or his employer. When someone is hurt during the course of their employment, workers' compensation ensures they are automatically entitled to several benefits, including payments for medical care and loss wages. No showing of fault is required. In return for these automatic benefits, workers are not permitted to sue co-workers or their employers. As such, we would not be suing Paul or his employer directly, but the multinational corporation that defectively designed and sold the lathe that Carlos was operating. Because unscrupulous factory owners will occasionally remove safety features to increase employee productivity, to protect workers the makers of industrial machines are required to design the parts of those machines to be tamper-proof.

After we sued the manufacturer of the industrial lathe, we learned there had been forty-five similar events with the same machines throughout the country that the manufacturer knew about, including one that blinded a man. That man had even brought a lawsuit, but the industrial lathe machine manufacturer tried to bury their multimillion-dollar settlement by not disclosing it to us. It was clear that, rather than have a recall and fix the exact defect that blinded one worker, they chose to leave the machine as it was. The company stubbornly refused to make a forty-dollar fix on a $90,000 lathe. If they had, Carlos would not have died.

Economic and Non-Economic Losses

The industrial machine manufacturer was smart enough to know it would only turn a jury against it by trying to argue Carlos's death wasn't their fault. They refused to accept any liability until the trial began. After our engineering experts explained to the jury that the industrial machine manufacturer knew about their design defect and chose not to fix it, they offered to pay Martina the amount Carlos would have earned if he'd kept his job with them for the next twenty years. They thought it was a done deal—she was poor, she needed the money—but Martina had the strength and confidence to turn it down. She knew the company still had not repaired the machine. She knew that the same lathe with the same defect was currently being operated in other factories by other men just like Carlos. That made her angry, but rage wasn't the source of her determination. She knew Carlos would not have stayed in his entry-level job. He would have moved up the ranks. He would have wanted more for his sons. The ongoing loss of his income while the company delayed, denied, and defended against her claim made life even more of a struggle. The company thought the loss of income was the most significant loss her family had suffered. Martina knew that was the smallest part of her claim.

The law recognizes that the wrongful death of a person does more than just financial damage to the family that's been left behind. Martina was keenly aware of the emotional damage Carlos's death had done to his boys. They had been traumatized by the news on Christmas morning. They'd lost their innocence and their faith in their mother. And now they were fatherless. The boys would never receive the guidance and nurturing Carlos would have provided. Children who grow up without a father are at higher risk of everything from drug addiction to suicide. Carlos had wanted the best possible life for his children, and his death prevented the boys from receiving his contributions to help make it possible.

Even though she never complained, Martina also felt the added stress of being a widow and a single parent to their boys. Carlos had been her best friend, lover, and husband, and with his death, she'd lost all three. To make ends meet, she would need to pick up a second job that would take more time away from her kids and move in with her mother-in-law, taking the boys out of their school district to one that wasn't as good. The truth was that the industrial machine manufacturer of the lathe that killed Carlos had wronged Martina and her sons, and that created a debt. Now the company was trying to set the value of what they owed.

The Right to Value the Damage

In an upscale antique store, imagine someone walking around who picks up a music box to play with. He cranks the handle but, while he's listening to the tune, spots a vintage record player—an old Victrola with the huge brass bell. Excited and not taking his eyes off his new find, he puts the music box down on a sofa arm instead of its display stand and then knocks it off and steps on it. When the shopkeeper hurries over to inspect the damage, the man impatiently agrees he broke the antique and offers the store owner twenty dollars.

"But it was worth two hundred dollars," the shopkeeper argues.

"It's not worth anything now," the man points out. "I'm offering more than anyone else would pay for it."

The person who does the damage doesn't get to determine how much damage they've done. Yet, that's what the defense lawyers in wrongful death and catastrophic injury cases regularly try to do. In this case, they set the "replacement price" for Carlos at a lowball estimate of what he would earn, without considering raises, over what remained of his working life. But in the same way that the clumsy shopper wasn't offering twenty dollars of justice but $180 of injustice, the manufacturing company was trying to set the value of what they'd taken from Carlos's wife and children.

When a defendant has taken responsibility for the harm they've done, the most usual reason a case goes to trial is a disagreement over what is required to make the injured party whole. Martina wanted to do all she could to make sure the manufacturing company (and every other company that operated the defective lathe) thought long and hard before they decided not to spend the forty dollars needed to fix their machines. Even more, she wanted to honor Carlos's intention to provide financial security for his boys.

Had her case been decided by a jury, I think the verdict they returned would have included (as the amount of the McDonald's coffee verdict did) additional money designed to punish the company for ignoring previous issues. I suspect the company thought the same thing because it made Martina a record offer that Martina accepted in the middle of the jury trial.

Settlements

Because I'm paid on contingency, and because that payment is a percentage of the final settlement amount, I had a financial incentive to suggest Martina hold out for more. But I have a responsibility to act in my clients' best interest, not my own, and it's always my clients' choice whether to settle or let a jury issue a verdict.

I told Martina that I believed the jury would likely return a higher verdict than the amount the company was offering her, but there was no guarantee. I counseled her to think about the long-term emotional consequences of accepting the settlement. I did not want her to feel pressured into accepting a settlement from the company that had caused her so much grief, anguish, and damage. On the other hand, if it was on her terms and gave her some closure, settling might be the right outcome for her and the boys.

Money is never the point, but it can and does make a difference. It can help people find closure, and it can go some distance toward making up the incalculable loss of a spouse and father. Money would not bring back Carlos, and some may think, *What's the point?* Our justice system is based on money as justice. In less civilized times, people lived by "eye for an eye" justice, where the same harm that was caused was imposed upon the wrongdoer. Thankfully our society has evolved, and an injured person's right to money justice is guaranteed in the Seventh Amendment of the Bill of Rights.

Martina had sued the company that designed and sold a defective machine that predictably killed Carlos, and she believed he would have wanted her to do all she could to make sure his death didn't cost their sons the better life he'd wanted for them. Plus, she told me, she knew other husbands and fathers operated other defective lathes in other factories. She didn't want another family to suffer the way hers had. By having the courage to bring her case seeking to hold a multinational multibillion-dollar company accountable for their choice to prioritize money over safety, Martina, like every other plaintiff I've represented, was providing a critical public service.

CHAPTER 5

A Public Service

Rachel is one of the strongest and most compassionate people I know. She manages to combine real warmth with a steeliness that's formidable but not intimidating. She's exactly the kind of woman you'd want for support when things get tough.

At forty-two, she went back to school and got a degree in psychology, specializing in grief counseling. Her teenage son had died the year before of leukemia, and she'd been stunned to find how little professional help was available for parents dealing with the loss of a child. She'd already written two books when I met her and helped hundreds of grieving parents and siblings.

I've always considered myself very fortunate to have a career that gives me a strong sense of purpose that helps people in my community. I recognized that same fire in Rachel. She was confident, energetic, and direct. "I know enough about grief," she told me, "to understand that guilt is unavoidable, and I know the difference between guilt and shame. When Dylan died, the guilt I felt was terrible, even though I knew I wasn't responsible for his illness and had done absolutely everything I could to help him fight and then accept it.

"After he died, I felt a duty to turn my grief and loss into something that could help others, but this is different. I have the same sense of responsibility, but I'm ashamed. It was hard for me to come see you because I almost can't stand to tell you what happened. It's almost like I'm doing penance even though I know I didn't do anything wrong. Just like with Dylan, I know I did the best I could."

She looked at me with clear, bright eyes. "I'm not an idealist," she said. "I don't expect the world to be fair. I don't even expect people to do what they say they will. I always do my research, and I always follow up. I don't avoid hard conversations. When my father died and my mother wanted to sell their house and move to Florida, we had a very candid talk. I told her I wouldn't move with her. I had two children who'd lost their brother, and they needed as much stability as I could provide for them. Mom understood her move would make it harder for me to help her out as she aged. Still, she'd found a retirement community she was excited about, and she wanted the sunshine.

"I think she made the right call. She was very happy there and made friends with people who really enriched her life. Then she had a stroke. I wanted to bring her back to Boston, but she wouldn't hear of it. She said if missing her friends didn't kill her, the winters would." Rachel shook her head, smiling. "She was a tough lady, but she was right. She would have hated it here, and I wasn't qualified to give her the kind of rehabilitative care she needed after the stroke.

"I found a Florida handyman to add a wheelchair ramp and widen the doors in Mom's house, and I started working on finding her a home health aide. I was so frustrated when insurance wouldn't cover someone to check on Mom twice a week. It would, however, cover a nursing home—one equipped with the handrails and lower counters we would have needed to retrofit her house with. I did the research and put together a shortlist. Then I flew down to visit them with Mom."

Rachel laughed. "It felt like an upside-down version of the trips she'd taken me on years ago to look at colleges. Now, I was grilling the administrators and she was the one embarrassed by all the questions. And we went on the same kind of campus tour—the rec room, the grounds, a single and a double residence room. The biggest difference was when we visited a dining hall, Mom would make at least one new friend. I'd been too shy as a high school student to introduce myself to college kids.

"Of the places we visited, one was the clear favorite. It was the most expensive, but we made it work. I flew back the next weekend and helped her get moved in. It was hard to leave her—harder than it had been to leave my kids in their freshman dorms. She was my mother. I owed her so much."

Rachel's voice trailed off. Something in her eyes told me she was seeing her mother as she had been on the day they'd moved her into the nursing home. Rachel pulled herself back to the present. "I put a nanny cam in her room," she told me. "And I could see almost right away that the facility was understaffed. Mom needed help using the toilet, and sometimes they kept her waiting so long she'd roll herself over to the bookcase and turn the camera off. She didn't want her child to see her wet herself. I'm almost fifty, but I'm 'the child' because she's the parent." Rachel laughed, then sobered quickly. "*Was* the parent," she corrected herself. "I complained to management at least twice a week, but I was stuck, and they knew it. I'd paid up front for three months of Mom's care."

When we eventually took the nursing home to court, this *quid pro quo* arrangement was part of Rachel's case. Quid pro quo translates from Latin as "what for what." It's used to describe any arrangement where one side agrees to do something in exchange for something (usually money). Rachel had fulfilled her side of the exchange by paying what she'd agreed to pay for her mother's care, but the nursing home had not honored its side. Rather than invest adequate monies to ensure proper staffing levels, the nursing home owners chose to increase their profits and neglect their residents by understaffing the facility.

Eldercare

The struggle to care for aging parents is not a bad problem to have. My mother died at fifty-six, and I appreciated my father more as time passed. To most people, it only seems right to do for our parents when they're old what they did for us when we were young. But there are significant differences. Infants weigh a lot less than even very frail elderly people, and they're less fragile. Without training or specialized equipment, the simple act of lifting someone from the bed can be a hazard to both people.

For many families, a nursing home is the best answer. Properly equipped nursing homes have handrails along every wall and supports on both sides of every toilet. Qualified staff members are trained to help the elderly transfer from bed to chair or chair to toilet. An onsite kitchen staffed with dieticians can ensure everyone's getting enough of the right kind of food, and there are also opportunities to socialize and exercise. Good nursing homes can extend a person's life and improve its quality. Bad ones can be fatal.

As we age, our skin thins and becomes increasingly fragile. At the same time, we also often lose physical strength. This is a dangerous combination. People who can't stand up or reposition themselves without help end up sitting in the same position for long periods. This causes constant pressure on specific contact points, which quickly blister if the skin is thin. Blisters caused in this way are called pressure ulcers or bedsores, and they're as predictable as they are preventable.

Older people with thin skin who can't move without help will develop bedsores unless they're helped regularly to reposition themselves. Bedsores that aren't treated often become infected. If they still aren't treated, the infection can spread through the body. This poses a double threat to the person's life. Many elderly people are unable to survive such an infection. That's what had happened to Rachel's mom. An untreated bedsore led to an infection for which she was hospitalized and died. This was not a natural death. Rachel's mom died before her time.

A Flawed System

"I came to see you because the guilt is keeping me up at night," Rachel told me. "If Mom had simply had more help shifting positions or if someone had properly treated the sore on the small of her back, she would still be alive. How could they have not taken better care of her?"

Rachel accepted a tissue from me, wiped her eyes, and blew her nose. She took a slow, shaky breath. "I wanted to do something to honor Mom's memory," she said. "She was always so social, and she loved people so much, I thought she'd appreciate it if I did something for her friends at the nursing home. I wanted to make sure that none of them ever had to deal with the same thing, so I talked to the CNAs [certified nursing assistants] who took care of her, and that's why I'm here."

Anger flashed in Rachel's eyes. "Those women cared about Mom. They care about all the residents. They're doing what they can; there just aren't enough of them. The nursing home advertises a three-to-one resident-to-staff ratio on its website. It was one of the first criteria in my search for places Mom could go. It was a big part of why we were willing to pay more for the one we chose, but the CNA I talked to said she'd never worked a shift when there were six of them on the clock, and the place was always full. That's a seven-to-one ratio, more than twice what they promised."

Betrayal

The business model for most nursing homes depends on keeping every room and bed full. Their income is based on occupancy, not staffing levels or what they spend on their residents. In other words, the higher the ratio of residents to staff, the more money the owner makes. Residents (or Medicare in many cases) contract with these businesses to provide a certain level of care for an agreed-on price, but all too often, the nursing home doesn't keep up its end of the bargain, and the elderly residents are neglected and sometimes pay for the shortfall with their lives.

"I just feel terrible," Rachel told me.

I've seen this happen so many times that I was able to coach Rachel a little bit. She couldn't quite name the feeling that was coloring her grief, but I recognized it. She had trusted the nursing home to care for her mother, but they had neglected her mom and betrayed her trust. Betrayal is almost always a part of the mix of emotions people suffer when their elderly parents are neglected.

In fact, betrayal operates almost as an over-theme in most cases of wrongful death and catastrophic injury, even in something as relatively ordinary as a car crash. When we get into our cars every day, each of us trusts that the other drivers on the road will obey the traffic laws as we do. We trust that they'll stop at stop signs and yield the right-of-way. And when they don't—when another driver speeds or drives under the influence of drugs or alcohol or while distracted or sleepy, that trust is betrayed.

SIDEBAR

Almost every fatality and injury on the road is caused by one of these four factors. People driving at an appropriate speed who are not mentally impaired by drugs, alcohol or fatigue, and who are not distracted very rarely hurt or kill anyone while driving. Of the factors behind most crashes, the one people respect and understand the least is distraction. I've seen the terrible consequences of tuning a radio, arguing with a passenger, or glancing at a cell phone. They are invariably life-altering where they're not fatal. Please, learn from my experience before you're forced into your own. When you get behind the wheel, drive with your full attention, at a safe speed, and free of the cognitive impairments caused by alcohol, illegal drugs, and some prescription medications.

To develop betrayal as a trial theme, I take jurors through its three steps: trust, vulnerability, and violation. Ottie trusted the housing complex management to provide a safe place for her and Joe to live. David trusted the streets of his city were a safe place to walk. Lily and her family trusted that drivers on their quiet suburban cul-de-sac would pay attention to the road. Carlos trusted the manufacturer of the lathe he was operating would design a safe piece of machinery. Rachel trusted the retirement home to provide her mother with the care she'd paid for.

The second component of betrayal is the one people most often miss. It's the relationship between trust and vulnerability. Without trust, we'd all necessarily exist in a constant state of hypervigilance, unable to do anything beyond trying to keep ourselves safe. Because we trust other drivers to stop at a red light, when we do the same, we relax a little, making ourselves vulnerable to the drunk driver flying up the road behind us. We become vulnerable when we walk up and down the aisles of a store looking at what's on the shelves rather than constantly scanning the floor ahead for spills or cracks. We expect a defect-free place to walk and become vulnerable by looking at the signs and products on the shelves. We all expect, and deserve, sidewalks to be free of defects too.

Ottie's trust in the security system made her and Joe vulnerable to the criminals who attacked them. David's trust in companies properly inspecting their trucks made him vulnerable when he stepped outside, as did Lily, as do all of ours.

The final feature of betrayal comes from the violation of our trust and the exploitation of our vulnerability. Or, as Rachel put it, "They ripped us off! We were paying for a three-to-one ratio and getting a five-to-one, and even after Mom died, they're still doing the same thing, cheating the government and the other residents out of what they're paying for, and that's just not right. It's fraud."

I agreed with Rachel, and I understood her desire to look out for the wellbeing of her mom's friends who were still being cheated by the nursing home. I told her we could sue the nursing home and hope it would teach them a lesson. Being held liable for the death of Rachel's mother might make it expensive enough for them to change their business model. But that wasn't good enough for Rachel.

Class Actions

When a group of people has been harmed in the same way by the same company, it's possible to take that business to court on behalf of everyone it's harmed. Even though none of the other residents at the nursing home had suffered physical injuries such as infections from bedsores, they had been financially harmed by the nursing home's failure to live up to its side of the agreed-upon arrangement, the *quid pro quo*.

We took the nursing home to court on behalf of all its residents and got a hefty settlement, which was divided between each resident who paid for services they didn't get. Rachel's portion of the settlement was probably smaller than the judgment she would have gotten had she sued individually. It was more important to her that the class action lawsuit got the attention of other nursing homes. Knowing that her mother's death had changed the living conditions for her mother's friends helped Rachel deal with her guilt. She had performed a public service and made something good come out of something terrible.

The public service provided by holding a company accountable for its betrayals of trust isn't limited to class action cases. Ottie's action against her housing complex changed how it patrolled and secured the property. After David's death, the trucking company changed not only its policies, but its practices, as did many (but, sadly, not all) similar companies. The home services company that killed Lily moved the GPS units off their company trucks' dashboards, and Carlos's company finally paid the forty dollars to repair the defective lathe.

For Rachel, as for most people involved in wrongful death suits, closure comes from having gotten justice and protections for others. In catastrophic injury cases, the motivations are different, and the closure is more about the future than the past. Every case we've discussed up to this point has been a story about people left behind when someone they loved was killed by the greed or negligence of a big company. In the rest of the book, as we talk about catastrophic injury cases, we'll look at how money paid in damages becomes less symbolic and more practical, providing a foundation for the future rather than closure on the past.

CHAPTER 6

The Soul of the System

"You know," Ty told me the first time I met him, "people talk about a city's streets and cars like veins and blood—the flow of traffic, a blockage in a major artery, but I don't see it." Ty had never lived anywhere else, so he conceded it might be that way in other cities. But in New York, he told me the streets were tattooed on. The city wore its ever-changing snakes and spirals of asphalt on its surface, and they never reached its heart. Ty said he was sure New York had one, but the only pulse he felt on that August afternoon was his own.

The box truck he'd driven eight hours a day, six days a week for the last ten years didn't have air conditioning, and his shirt stuck to his back. He was getting a good breeze through the open window, though, doing fifty-five on the Van Wyck Expressway that runs through Queens out to JFK Airport. But he was late. Two hours earlier, an old man couldn't find his glasses to sign for his delivery and made Ty wait while he looked for them. Ty thought he could sign a touch screen with his eyes shut, but he didn't say anything. Glasses found, the signature looked like half of a badly made tent, and Ty left the place twenty minutes behind schedule. He hadn't been able to make up the time, but like his boss always said, he got paid for the delivery, not the driving.

On an elevated three-lane highway through New York City, traffic snarled in the heat, coming to a complete stop just three hundred yards shy of the long, clear exit-only lane that led to Ty's next delivery. He was already late, and the entry to the lane was close, but he couldn't squeeze around the box truck in front of him, and there was no shoulder. Ty felt every second of sitting still tick in his chest. Finally, the brake lights ahead flickered off then on again. Cars were starting to inch forward.

The exit-only lane got a little closer, but time kept ticking, moving forward faster than he was, each second making him later. *Just one more car length*, he thought. Then, *That's it, my brother!* as the box truck in front of him reached the entrance to the exit ramp and accelerated. Its driver was taking the same exit Ty needed! He pulled into the exit lane and stepped on the gas. The air started moving inside the truck once again. For a good quarter of a mile, he and the other box truck were both moving along at a healthy thirty-five to forty miles an hour, headed for the point where the exit-only lane separated from the highway and pulled right. Then everything happened at once.

For Ty, time slowed almost to a stop. He remembered every moment like a photo he'd stared at for hours. He remembered his thoughts like a calm conversation, although he couldn't have had more than a few seconds to think them. He thought, *That dude's hit his brakes. Hard. And he's angling left. Back onto the highway. Not to the right with the ramp. Why is he stopping at the end of the exit lane and not going down the ramp?*

Ty hit his own brakes. He thought, *There's two car-lengths between us, and it's going to be gone before I can stop. I don't want to hit him. I don't know why he stopped so hard so fast—maybe there's a wreck. Maybe somebody's on the road. If I hit him, I could knock him into whatever's in front of him.*

He thought, *I can't swerve left. There are three lanes of packed traffic standing still that I'd plow into. I gotta not hurt those people.*

There's some space between that stopped box truck and the guard rail. Not much. I'd hit it for sure.

Better me than them.

But it's a fifteen-foot drop if I go through the guardrail.

If I go through the rail, I'll die.

Maybe kill someone on the road underneath.

Death's in every direction.

No good options.

No safe path.

No—

Still standing on his brakes, doing everything he could to avoid the crash, Ty angled his box truck to the right, hoping to get around the stopping truck ahead with damage only to the guard rail and his own truck.

After that, time went from a slowed-down film to single snapshots for him. There wasn't enough room to squeeze by. *Almost made it.* The front left corner of Ty's truck hit the rear right corner of the stopped box truck. The metal bumper of the box truck pushed the walls of the driver's compartment in on him. *Screaming.* It took off his left leg just below the knee.

Three days later, he shivered, remembering the pain and the sight of it. *Just gone.*

Amputation

The surgeons took extraordinary care trying to save Ty's knee because they knew the difference those few inches can make. Above-the-knee amputations are more medically complex, and because a leg gets most of its power from the thigh muscles, a below-the-knee amputation that leaves those muscles intact allows the leg to retain most of its strength. Below-the-knee prosthetics are much easier to walk with and require less energy to manipulate than the above-the-knee ones. With two prosthetic joints (an ankle and a knee), regaining the ability to walk becomes a more difficult, lengthy, and painful process with above-the-knee amputees.

Ty was only twenty-eight when I met him, and the crash was only a week in the past. He hadn't started rehabilitation yet, and he was scared. He said the rest of his life didn't sound like something worth fighting to save. The doctors had explained that he would need months of physical therapy and that, although he would be able to drive an automatic vehicle again, he'd never be able to carry heavy deliveries up driveways or into buildings. Young and single, a week earlier, he'd thought he had it made with everything to look forward to. Now, he couldn't imagine a future he'd find acceptable.

He could, however, imagine the medical bills associated with the cost of his care. He was terrified his parents would spend everything they'd saved for their retirement on his recovery.[7] He couldn't take the guilt of ruining their lives on top of everything else. He knew he'd heard somewhere that all rear-end wrecks are the fault of the person behind, but he couldn't make that square with what had happened. How could this have been his fault? He'd done everything he could. There was no option that would have ended with a better outcome.

On only the second day after his sixteen-hour surgery, Ty started making phone calls, but every lawyer he talked to said the same thing: He had no case. Ty needed a lawyer, but first, he needed a pep talk.

At the hospital, I told Ty that I'd represented many amputees and whether or not he had a case, I'd share their experiences with him. I told him that he was facing the hardest days and promised him that things would get better. I told him about Simon, the seventeen-year-old high school football player who had been on suicide watch in the days after losing his leg. Today, he's at college studying accounting and learning to paint. I told Ty that Simon called me recently and shared that he was grateful for the wreck that took his leg as it left him with a very different life—one with purpose and clarity.

I also shared the story of another twenty-eight-year-old man who was riding his motorcycle when a car turned left in front of him without any warning. He, too, lost his left leg. He, too, thought his future was bleak. I shared how I helped him get to the right prosthetic expert, how hard he worked in his

---

7   Since Ty was working at the time of the crash, workers' compensation paid all of his past and future medical bills, including the most basic prosthetic device.

rehabilitation, and how just five short years after his crash, I watched him dance at his wedding. The future is hard to see from a hospital bed with one of your limbs missing, and I needed Ty to know that he would get better, and he would thrive once again.

SIDEBAR

Unlike wrongful death cases, it's not unusual to hear people who've suffered a terrible injury say, a few years later, that they're grateful it happened. But I don't tell people this in the early days of their recovery. They wouldn't believe me, and they might take it as making light of their suffering.

Prosthetics

Because I keep up to date on the technological advancements in prosthetics, I could offer Ty a little perspective. The latest technology is excellent and advancing quickly. A company run by a double amputee MIT graduate is doing remarkable work. They supplied most of the devices used by the victims of the Boston Marathon bombing and are constantly improving the comfort and control of their prosthetics. Recently, they introduced an artificial skin that they can modify to match a photo of the person's limb before their injury—even down to any tattoos. Many prosthetics now have flexible, battery-powered joints that increase the distances amputees can walk comfortably. As I told Ty, there are special prosthetics for running, swimming, hiking, and more. A prosthetic is simply a mobility tool, and the activity determines which tool to use.

When I told Ty all this, he just shrugged and said, "Sounds expensive."

"Why don't you tell me what happened?" I suggested.

Exceptions to the Rules

When I heard Ty's story as I've outlined it here, including the fact that his call to me was the last he'd planned to make before giving up, I was glad I'd taken the time to come and speak with him. I explained that the other lawyers hadn't really been mistaken about rear-end wrecks but that I was willing to give it a shot. I understood that it was risky, but he was so young and, in my estimation, had done nothing wrong. I was willing to stand with him even though I knew we might lose.

In Chapter 4, I pointed out that being paid on contingency creates a strong incentive for lawyers to take only those cases they're confident they can win. In most cases, that's true. In Ty's case, I was willing to make an exception. I told Ty we might not win, but we wouldn't go down without a hell of a fight.

Taking a wrongful death or catastrophic injury case to trial is slow, expensive, and time-intensive. I spend hundreds of person-hours and tens of thousands of dollars in advance, and my investment starts as soon as I take the case. In Ty's, we began a detailed investigation of the scene, getting witnesses' testimony from as many of the drivers sitting in the stopped traffic as we could find. We studied the police report, got aerial photos, and established there was no traffic ahead of the truck when its driver slammed on the brakes. That man was "one of those drivers" who ignores the rules of the road. He had gotten into the exit-only lane planning to gain a few car lengths on the people sitting at a standstill. He stopped short because he'd pushed as far ahead as he could get and wanted to cut back into the stopped traffic.

Ty had been using the exit lane as intended—to exit—and reasonably expected the driver ahead of him was doing the same. After all, everyone who wasn't exiting was stopped on the highway waiting their turn. A deeper investigation revealed that the other driver wasn't naturally as aggressive and discourteous as his actions that day would suggest. Like Ty and like the bucket truck driver in Chapter 3, he worked for a company that put its drivers under unreasonable time constraints. Their requirement that drivers make a certain number of deliveries per hour did not take traffic into account. The first major challenge was establishing that a rear-end crash is not always the rear-ending driver's fault. Careful reconstruction of the circumstances and conditions of the crash allowed us to meet it. The next challenge was finding the right jury.

The Art of Jury Selection

Because it depends on fair and impartial jurors, our legal system allows the lawyers on both sides to evaluate whether a potential juror can judge the facts of the case without bias or prejudice. The idea that a driver who hits a car from behind is always at fault isn't correct, and it isn't the law. It's a bias. Any potential juror who believed it was always the rear driver's responsibility to avoid a crash would have prejudged Ty before the trial started. We screened for that mistaken belief and had anyone who held it excused.

That was a fairly straightforward question, but I'm not always so blunt when questioning potential jurors. Sometimes, I imagine my questions seem quite odd. In Ty's case, I asked two questions that I imagine had potential jurors scratching their heads. The first was crafted to screen for people with experience driving in New York City. I posed the question this way, "Do you believe that driving in New York is different from driving in De Moines, Iowa?"

People who have no experience driving in New York might agree or disagree, but no one who's ever driven in the city thinks it's the same as driving anywhere else. This was an important point because I knew the defense would claim that Ty couldn't stop in time to avoid the wreck because he was following too closely behind the other box truck. I wanted to get out in front of that attack when I questioned him in a way the jury would understand.

At trial, I took Ty through his last hours as an able-bodied man. "Traffic is at a standstill," I reminded him. "You're almost to the exit-only lane. The truck in front of you pulls into it, opening up the space. You follow that truck into the exit-only lane. Why?"

"Because I was going to exit."

"Sure, isn't that what the lane is for?" I asked, underscoring the point. "You accelerate, and now you're following that truck with only two car lengths between you. Why so close?"

"Well," Ty said. "First, because I'm exiting. Second, because it's New York City."

That got a chuckle from the jury. Ty grinned and shrugged. "If you give much more space than that, some other guy is going to jump in there, you know? Pretty soon, you'll be going backward."

Everyone on the jury was nodding their heads. They'd driven in New York; they knew Ty's description was accurate. When the defense questioned Ty, they couldn't go after him too hard for tailgating without insulting New York drivers in general. Ty and the jury had that in common. I think it threw the defense for a loop. They'd never expected the jury to find their client even fractionally at fault, but it did. The jurors found the line-cutting truck 100 percent to blame for the wreck. "If he'd just stayed in the traffic like everyone else, that poor boy would still have his leg," one of the jurors said to me after the verdict.

Judges' Instructions

Judges tell jury members to make two distinct determinations—liability and damages. Liability answers who's at fault, whether the blame is shared and what the percentage split is. If the jury concludes the defendant bears some responsibility, the question of damages revolves around how much they should be required to pay for the damage they caused. My second slightly peculiar question posed during jury selection was asked with an eye to secure a significant verdict on damages. It was: "What kind of phone do you use?"

I asked this question knowing that one of the expert witnesses I planned to introduce would explain the history of prosthetic legs. She talked the jury through the evolution from literal peg legs made of wood and strapped to the thigh with leather straps through the development of an artificial, fully articulating ankle joint attached to a paddle-like foot that allowed amputees to wear a shoe and pants.

She explained other, more recent improvements and finally discussed the artificial leg Ty was currently wearing—its advances and drawbacks. When I asked her about the future, she beamed. "Technology is advancing so quickly!" she said. "We're on the brink of some very exciting improvements. They've recently introduced a prosthetic that houses a small battery that can replicate the lift we get from our feet when we walk. The next generation will integrate directly with Ty's nervous system. In ten years, he could have a leg which he could then learn to manipulate with his brain. The possibilities are hopeful."

In my summation at the end of the trial, I reminded the jury of the doctor's testimony and gave them an analogy for how technology evolves. "Think about your smartphone," I suggested. "Most of you are old enough to remember the old candy bar and flip phones that came before them. Some of you may even remember landlines, but let's not go back into ancient history.

Start with your first cell phone and think of it like a peg leg—very basic. Sure, it was mobile, but all it could do was make calls. Later developments added some primitive texting functions. The next models could handle email, and then smartphones came along and added music, maps, games, and all kinds of other apps. And they keep making improvements.

"Today, we're up to the iPhone 13, and we all know 14 isn't far behind. In a couple more years, there'll probably be an iPhone 20. Who knows what it will make possible? But the defense is telling you Ty shouldn't get a current-generation phone. That's too good for him. Even though he did nothing wrong and ended up an amputee, he only deserves an iPhone 2."

Because I'd asked during jury selection, I knew every jury member had a recent model Android or iPhone. I saw the comparison land. "I'm asking you to disagree with the defense," I told them. "Help Ty get a good prosthetic, equivalent to at least an iPhone 10, and ensure that later, as the technology advances, he'll be able to keep up. Take a minute to imagine the alternative. What if the defense told you what they're telling Ty—that you had to go back to an iPhone 2 forever? What would it be like to know that for the rest of your life, you had to stay with the phone you have now? You couldn't upgrade it.

"The first smartphone came out in 2007—less than fifteen years ago, and it was discontinued and replaced by the next model just a year later. Think about how much technology has progressed since then. The same kind of innovation is happening now with prosthetic devices. What's possible in the next fifteen years? Who knows, but Ty will have just turned forty.

"Doctors went to heroic lengths to save his knee because medical science understands that the ability to walk is critical to his quality of life. Even more critical than cell phones. I'm asking you to make sure Ty isn't stuck with his ability to walk controlled by flip-phone era technology. He's twenty-five years old. The verdict you deliver today will allow him access to the technology he'll depend on to walk for the rest of his life, for the next fifty years at least. Fifty years ago, phones were wired to the wall and operated by a dial. Push-button phones hadn't been invented yet. Don't hold Ty to such antiquated technology for something so important."

And they didn't.

We collected the maximum insurance available, and the jury voted to award Ty a record verdict. In doing this, they demonstrated that the rules that govern how we drive have real teeth and that their violation had severe consequences for people other than Ty. Rules without consequences are meaningless. The people of that jury showed that the rules have meaning, but Ty took another lesson from them as well. "You know," he told me, "I think I've found the city's heart."

I believe he had. The jury system is the soul of our democracy, and when jurors put people first, they're also its beating heart.

CHAPTER 7

Putting People First

My law firm has over fifty lawyers, but the most important people in the office are the ten people who handle our new case calls. They're all compassionate listeners who care deeply about every person who calls, whether we end up taking their case or not.

Our entire intake process is designed to be as painless as possible. Because we know that anyone who's calling us has already explained what happened to the police, to doctors, and to friends and family, we try to spare them having to give redundant accounts to us. One of our intake specialists listens to their story and, if there's a way we can help, sets up a meeting—in person or remotely—with one of our lawyers.

That first meeting often takes place at the hospital, and it's also designed to be extremely sensitive to the needs of people in crisis. When our lawyers talk to someone for the first time, we've already read and studied everything the potential client told our intake staff. We don't ask them to repeat themselves or relive what happened yet again. We simply confirm that someone was responsible for whatever tragedy they face.

Because I know the process of starting a lawsuit can be intimidating, we've produced hundreds of hours of free videos explaining every step in detail—from investigation to funds disbursement. Because I also know that people in such situations have enough to deal with and are usually feeling overwhelmed, we listen more than we talk. We also bring a packet of information with us, so they don't have to remember everything we tell them. At our first meeting, we explain that they'll never write us a check and that we only get a fee if we win. We provide the broad strokes of the timeline and experience they can expect.

The Investigation

Our firm employs twelve retired police officers. One of them often goes with the lawyer to their first meeting with a potential client so that we can begin our investigation as soon as we sign with the new client. After that, we tell our new clients to put all their legal worries out of their minds and focus on getting better. We will take care of everything else.

The first thing we do for a new client is to reach out to the insurance company of the person, people, or company responsible for what happened and ask them to do the right thing. Occasionally, they do. A young man who'd lost a foot in a motorcycle wreck once came to see me. The driver who'd cut him off in traffic had only the minimum required $25,000 of insurance, and when I called her insurance company, they offered the entire $25,000 immediately. I accepted the money on his behalf, handed it over, and didn't take a fee. Justice was not served, but he chose to accept it rather than go after the driver personally because he knew the crash was accidental.

> ### SIDEBAR
>
> We're not in the business of putting people out of their homes, so we rarely pursue individual people. But when a large company with millions of dollars in assets neglects its responsibility to stay adequately insured, we will pursue a claim in excess of available insurance to force the company to pay for the damage it caused.

More often, the insurance company balks, and we get to work acting as both information gatherers and information providers. We collect information from medical providers, the police, and any witnesses. We deliver that information to the insurance company and give them another chance to do the right thing.

Sometimes, the insurance company, faced with all the data we provide, will offer the full amount of insurance available at this point, particularly if it's substantially below the amount of damage done. For example, knowing one of its insured has done $10,000,000 worth of injury and has only a $500,000 policy, the insurance company might offer the full amount or close to it. In these instances, we verify that the insurance company is telling the truth about the maximum available coverage. We then explain the situation to our clients, giving them the choice to accept the insurance settlement or to directly pursue the person or company for additional damages.

Most often, the insurance companies launch into the 3D dance I mentioned in Chapter 1. They deny responsibility, delay making any agreement or paying any settlement, and defend the case to avoid doing exactly what their insured had been paying them to do. That's when we begin litigation. We're effectively asking a jury to force whoever is responsible for the damage to pay since they won't do it voluntarily. What has, until now, been a claim becomes a lawsuit—a summons and complaint. It comes to this because the insurance company has refused to act responsibly by offering the right amount of money for the damages their insured caused. People who are seriously injured prefer their health over any money they may recover. In fact, in my thirty-three years of representing people who've lived through the unimaginable, I've only had one client who told me the money was worth it.

The Exception That Proves the Rule

Frank was in his late sixties with two adult children—a son and a daughter. His wife had died while the youngest was still in college, but both "kids" were doing well. They had jobs nearby and were starting families of their own.

Frank was a veteran who'd been injured overseas, but he'd lived a remarkable life from his wheelchair. After his injury, with his wife's support, he quickly accepted his new constraints, got a job, and moved up from tech support to management. He was starting to think seriously about retirement.

His company had recently bought a new building and asked Frank's team to work half-days in the new place. Had the construction company followed the building regulations, it would have carefully inspected its work before giving the occupancy okay, but they didn't. The project was late and over budget, and they cleared Frank's team to move in a few days late on a Wednesday.

Frank worked a few hours before he had to use the restroom. He wheeled into the oversized "handicapped" stall and started to transfer from his wheelchair to the toilet seat. The seat wasn't installed correctly and flew off. It pitched Frank onto the floor, breaking a single bone in his neck and instantly paralyzing him. He could turn his head and raise or lower his chin, and that was it. He was paralyzed and, initially, unable to breathe on his own. After months in the hospital, he transferred to the specialized nursing home where he spent almost a year before he was finally able to leave and move in with his oldest son. I visited Frank several times while he was in the nursing home, and each time he told me how much he missed his dog.

I went to see him again the day before he was due to go home. He said he thought it would be nice to get out of the kind of institutional surroundings he'd been in for the last year and a half, but what he was looking forward to most was his reunion with Lester, his dog. He'd gotten to see his kids, he explained. They'd come to visit him every week, but he desperately missed his dog. His son David had even tried to smuggle Lester in to see him, but Labradors aren't small or famous for their subtlety.

Three years later, when I handed Frank his check for several millions of dollars, I asked about Lester. Frank grinned. "I'm a pain in his tail," he said. "The old boy won't leave my side."

It was true, Lester lay on the floor, his head on his paws, his sleek black side pressed against one wheel of Frank's chair. "Watch this," he told me and called the dog.

Lester's ears stood up, and he raised his head.

"Go on, boy." Frank waved toward the kitchen. "Let's go." Frank put his chin on the lever that activated the wheelchair. "Out of the way now."

Lester didn't move. Frank started to roll forward slowly, and I could see what was about to happen. "You're going to run over his tail."

Frank stopped. "I know it. Lester knows it too, but he'll take the pain rather than let any space come between us." Frank laughed. "You know what they say about old dogs and new tricks."

"You've learned a few in the last couple of years," I said.

"Yeah, suppose so." His eyes shifted as his son came into the room.

"It's David, Dad," the young man said to his father—then to me, "He doesn't like not being able to see what's behind him."

Frank grinned. "Andrew's brought us a lot of money."

"Wasn't worth it." David sat down beside his dad.

"Sure, it was."

I've delivered checks between hundreds of thousands to millions of dollars to people, and I always ask them: If we could travel back in time to the day before whatever event caused their injuries and I told them what would happen from the fateful moment up to the one when I delivered the check, would they change it? Everyone has always said they would, and the larger the amount, the faster they say they would have stayed home or left the country, anything to avoid the catastrophe that the money they'd just gotten was supposed to make right. But here was Frank, who'd endured six surgeries and two years of treatment and rehabilitation away from his family and his dog, saying it was worth it? I was stunned. David was furious.

"How can you say that, Dad?"

Fifteen years later, I still remember David's shrug. "Now I'll have something to leave you and your sister when I go. I didn't have much of a nest egg, and after all the medical bills, none of it's left."

"Dad," David said. "If there's one thing all of this has taught me, it's that none of that matters. We all spent what we had saved. We wanted to. Getting you back was all we cared about. Think about it; you wouldn't take that much money to have the same thing happen to Lester, would you?"

"No," Frank said, "But—" He turned to me. "You understand, don't you? We work hard to make a better life for our kids. Living through the last couple of years was a lot of work, but it's worth it."

The Impact of Attitude

Frank's quality of life was fairly poor. He could do almost nothing for himself and needed full-time nursing care, but he could still see a way to find something meaningful in what had happened to him. The resilience of the human spirit always inspires me, and I've come to recognize it as perhaps the single most powerful predictor of how (or whether) people will recover from whatever tragedy has fallen into their lives.

As I've said, I almost always meet people during their worst days. They're all distraught, overwhelmed, frightened, and in pain. Many are angry. Some are suicidal. Most express some faith that things will (or, at least, might) get better. It makes all the difference.

Human beings are prediction machines. For an easy example of what I mean, if I say, "two plus two," my guess is that your mind has already supplied "equals four." Of course, you didn't know what I was planning on saying. It might have been "plus seven" or "is more than a sum of its parts," but your brain can't resist filling in the most predictable next piece. Human beings also really like to be right. If you've predicted an outcome, you're likely to work toward making it a reality. This is why I've learned to pay close attention to the outcomes people predict for critically injured loved ones or families that have suffered a terrible loss.

Most people are remarkably resilient. Even when situations are dire, most people will tell me, "I know he'll pull through," or "She's a fighter; she'll walk again." When a family member has been wrongfully killed, they'll say, "We're going to be okay," or "We'll get through this somehow." Sometimes they'll add, "I can't see it from here," or "I don't know how." Occasionally, however, a distraught parent, spouse, or child of a badly injured person will tell me, "He's going to die," or "There's no way he can recover," and when they do, I believe them.

If you're reading this book in the middle of a crisis, I'd like to encourage you to work hard for optimism. I know it's difficult, and I know things may be very dark right now, but if you can have faith in light to come, you'll help yourself and others make it to better days ahead.

It's been my experience that people who predict the worst do so, not out of some kind of personal negativity, but because their pasts have taught them that terrible things can and do happen. A desire to break that cycle is part of why I always come equipped with stories of people who have suffered and survived something similar. It's also part of what made Frank's positive spin on becoming paralyzed remarkable to me. He'd already suffered life-altering injuries. He knew there were wounds from which we cannot recover, but he still saw a silver lining from the darkest of clouds.

Prediction and the Jury

It is this brighter future I paint for the jury. I don't try to play on their sympathy or paint my clients as victims, no matter how victimized they might have been. That is the past. The jury can't undo it. A jury can (and does) determine what kind of future my clients can access.

Frank spent ten months in a trauma ICU before he was moved into the rehabilitation hospital where I met him. At the time, he couldn't imagine life at home with his son and his dog, but I described it to him and promised he'd get there one day. It's part of my job and my moral responsibility to show my clients the positive outcome I predict for them. I do the same for the jury.

I told the jurors about Frank's traumas and the losses, the surgeries, and pain. I told them about the deep appreciation Frank had for the simple pleasure of talking to Lester and telling the old dog to move out of the way, knowing he wouldn't listen. I told the jury the truth—that the last chapter of Frank's story was in their hands. Frank's mouth-controlled wheelchair, his nursing care, and the additional surgeries he would require were expensive.

Companies today are working on a kind of wearable, external skeleton that might allow Frank to walk to the mailbox one day. If the rapidly evolving technology of brain-operated devices opened other possibilities for Frank's increased independence, they'd be out of his financial reach unless the jury took steps to see that they weren't. "There's a better and a worse possible future for Frank and Lester," I told the jury. "And there's a direct relationship to the size of the verdict you return. You can vote for a better life for Frank." And they did.

The Pursuit of Happiness

The rights to life, liberty, and the pursuit of happiness are at the core of those our country was established to provide. No one can take another person's life or kidnap them without severe consequences. Even the government holds itself to a very high standard of proof with multiple chances at appeal before executing a criminal or putting one in jail. But every one of the defendants who comes before a jury in a wrongful death or serious injury case is trying to convince them that it's okay that they've taken away another human being's ability to pursue happiness.

On the most basic level, every one of my clients is suing over their loss of enjoyment of life. Frank could still have a good day, but he could no longer pursue happiness the way he had before.

Without Frank, Lily, David, and Carlos, their spouses, children, family, and friends would carry a lifelong loss and their grief over it. They could and would be happy again, but for each of them, their American right to the pursuit of happiness had been badly interfered with.

Every case is bigger than the individual people standing before the jury. It's also about the Constitution of our country, and we ask them to uphold its values and the principles we, as a nation, claimed our independence to promise our people. I ask the jury to honor that promise and protect our most deeply held rights. They usually do, and it's their actions that tell us who we are as Americans.

The same is true of every plaintiff, defendant, and lawyer. What we do says who we are.

CHAPTER 8

Actions Prove Identity

Tina was exhausted. "I have three kids, and one of them is seventy-something," she told me. "I know it sounds like a bad joke, but one of my kids is my mother, and here's the punchline: I had just moved in with her after my marriage ended to have some help with my kids."

Martha, Tina's mother, had been an outgoing and energetic woman. Early one morning in spring, after a long and icy winter, she decided to ride her bicycle to the grocery store to pick up eggs for her grandchildren's breakfast. The neighborhood streets had bike lanes, and Martha pedaled up the long hill and coasted down. She pulled into the store parking lot and rolled over several speed bumps.

Speed bumps, we later learned, are surprisingly fragile and easy to damage with the blade of a snowplow. Any city street or private property that uses them is required to maintain them in good repair. Unfortunately for Martha, the grocery store had used a discount contractor, and the speed bumps in its parking lot were poorly made and not maintained.

That spring morning, she pedaled her bike over several speed bumps before hitting one from which a large section of concrete had broken off the back half. The store had removed the detached piece several weeks earlier but hadn't taken any action to fill the hole the missing concrete created. Had they examined it with an eye on safety, they would have seen that it created a dangerous situation for anyone going over the speed bump from the "good side." Not only was the back half of the mound torn away, but a chunk of the asphalt had also been gouged out. Martha went easily up the sloped side of the speed bump, and then, without warning and unable to see the hole, her bike plunged from off the sheer break and into the rain-filled hole on the far side. It threw Martha over the handlebars and onto the pavement.

"There were only two other times I ever saw her stand still," her daughter told me. "She was pretty quiet for about a year after Dad died, and before that, she'd had a hip replacement that slowed her down for a month or so. She had a beautiful garden, and she'd mostly let me carry the bags of mulch or heavier pots around, but if I weren't there, she wouldn't let it stop her. Nothing stopped her." Tina took an unsteady breath. "I've let that garden go to seed," she said. "I just don't have the time to take care of it too. Or the heart. Ella—she's my youngest—she still goes out there sometimes. I think she blames herself for what happened to Mom."

After she divorced, Tina had moved in with her mother. Martha had insisted. "She said she'd been lonely after Dad died, and she wanted to see her grandbabies more, but that woman hasn't been lonely a day in her life. She wanted me to move in because she knew I needed the help. When I moved in, I swore it was just for a couple of months, but we got along so well, I never felt like I needed to move out, and every time I brought it up, the kids just howled. They loved their afternoons with her." Tina paused. "Not so much anymore," she said.

I HOPE WE NEVER MEET

"Mom's short-tempered now, and sometimes she says things that are just plain mean. The girls don't want to be around her, and I can't say I blame them. She's frustrating on a whole lot of levels. I don't know what to tell them. I mean, it's not their granny anymore, even though it is. Mom looks the same, and she still talks all the time, but she's not the same person. I'm not sure they even remember what Mom is really like—*was* really like. It's hard to think of her as the same person when she acts so differently. It's almost like she died that day and sometimes—" Tina blinked back tears. "Sometimes I wish she had."

"I understand," I told her. "In my mind, traumatic brain injury cases are wrongful deaths. I would never stand up in front of a jury and say, 'This is the equivalent of a wrongful death case,' but I think of it that way. The body of your mother is still with you, but what made her who she was—her essence—is gone."

Tina nodded. "It's like a reverse ghost."

"You lost your mother," I said. "But you never got to have a funeral or say goodbye."

I told Tina that she would probably go through the entire grief cycle over losing her mom to the traumatic brain injury that had altered her personality so radically.

"Great, so I get to double-dip?" Tina barked a laugh. "Once now and again when Mom dies? It's like there are two Marthas—pre-wreck Martha and post-wreck Martha, and I have to lose both, one at a time."

I nodded. I've handled multiple traumatic brain injury cases and seen their devastating impact on families. I could only imagine how difficult it must be for Tina to lose the mother she counted on in that way.

"I'm trying hard not to feel resentful," Tina said. "I know it's not her fault. The doctors told me that everything—the way she can't control her emotions anymore or remember things or get organized—it's all part of the same brain system. It's what they call 'executive functioning,' except Mom's doesn't, you know, function. I can't leave her alone anymore. She wanders off, leaving the stove on and the front door wide open. And I can't take her with me, even when I do the grocery shopping. She shoplifts candy bars. She can't remember anything I ask her to do. She's physically fine, but she needs full-time care, and I have to work!"

Tina paused for a moment, collecting herself. "Mom would hate it if she knew she was making things harder instead of easier on us, but she doesn't realize she's changed. I try to tell her she's suffering from a traumatic brain injury. Everyone else can see it, but she'll look you in the face and say she's as good as she ever was. I tried to get her health insurance to pay for someone to watch her so I could go back to my job, but that's what Mom told the guy who called, 'Good as I ever was!' So, of course, he said she didn't need the help. He acted like I was trying to scam them for babysitting."

Traumatic Brain Injury (TBI)

As I told Tina, the difficulty with brain trauma is that it's less visible than damage done to other parts of the body. It doesn't show up like scars on skin or on X-rays like a broken bone. Often, it isn't even visible on MRIs or CAT scans. "The grocery store has a responsibility to maintain and repair the speed bumps in their parking lot and make it a safe place for people to walk, drive, or bike. They didn't do what they were supposed to, but if we sue them, their insurance company's lawyers are going to say your mom has completely recovered," I warned her. "But there are ways to prove that the damage is long-term and permanent."

It can be challenging to prove that brain trauma has caused changes in a person's mood, behavior, and decision-making processes in part because it's difficult to determine a person's "baseline." We rarely have a good picture of "before" to compare with the "after." People don't routinely get brain scans the way we get our blood pressure checked at each visit to a doctor. Worse, there aren't good metrics to measure personality even after an injury. To quantify the loss of a person's mental abilities, we have to work backward from the facts we can establish about them before they were hurt. To explain how it works, I told Tina about Tony, another of my clients with a traumatic brain injury.

Tony had been a young man with a bright future. In the last semester of his senior year in high school and already registered to start at MIT in the fall, he had taken a summer job working construction. One afternoon, he was on a building site when a pipe fell fifteen feet from a scaffold and hit him on the side of his hard hat and unprotected shoulder. His mother called us because Tony was struggling with neck and upper back pain that wasn't resolving.

When I went to see him, he was resting on a sofa in the family room with the curtains drawn. I sat across from him and noticed his squint almost immediately. When his mom came in with a coffee for us, he flinched at the light. "What's going on?" I asked him.

"Bright lights hurt my eyes," Tony told me. "Ever since the accident, I'm just a lot more comfortable in dark rooms. They're more restful somehow."

I knew right away that Tony had suffered a brain injury in addition to the broken collar bone. The long-term effects of head trauma can take anywhere from a few days to several years to fully manifest, and it's frighteningly easy for them to go undiagnosed.

With Tony, we were lucky. We didn't have neuropsychological studies or scans of his brain from before his injury, but we did have his grades, SAT scores, and college entrance essays. We knew he'd had executive functioning skills strong enough to keep track of his work, school, sports, and social schedules. This helped us establish a baseline level of functioning before the injury that put him in the top 8 percent of kids his age. On the assessments he took later, his scores dropped from the eightieth to the sixtieth percentile.

Of course, the insurance lawyers for the construction company tried to point out that at 60 percent, Tony was still functioning like an average person his age, implying that was good enough. They brushed aside the loss of one-fourth of his cognitive ability and the fact that it meant he could no longer do MIT-level work.

Tony lost the future he'd been planning and the chance to realize his full potential. He was also unable to concentrate at the same level he had before. When he studied, he remembered less and needed more frequent breaks. The quality of his writing went down, and he lost some of the physical coordination that had made him a star athlete.

Finally, and most upsetting to him, he lost friends. Most of the kids he'd been closest to left for college and were already sophomores by the time he was able to go back to school. And his personality changed too. He was no longer the easygoing kid grinning out at you from the pages of his yearbook. He was temperamental with friends and disruptive in the classroom.

Assessment of TBI

Lawyers like to put numbers on things, but not everything in life is easily measured. Even the cognitive assessments neuropsychologists conduct aren't like an equation. If different people do the same equation accurately, they get the same answer. Two qualified and unbiased assessors are more likely than not to score thinking tests differently.

To further complicate things, doctors (like lawyers, I'm told) have a different relationship with language than ordinary people do. (I, for example, will almost always say "almost always." I almost never say "never.") Doctors use "traumatic brain injury" to cover everything from a concussion to widespread brain damage, coma, and death. Inside that very broad category of TBI, doctors grade an injury's severity as mild, moderate, or severe, but with an interesting twist. The determination is made primarily on how long the person reports having been knocked out (unconscious), which is something that can't always be accurately estimated.

Martha had gone over her handlebars and landed headfirst. Luckily, another shopper saw her and called 911 immediately. A helicopter quickly got her to the local Level I trauma center (the most advanced ranking), where doctors put her into a medically induced coma and kept her in the hospital for ten days. But because she had only been initially unconscious for a few minutes, her diagnosis was "mild traumatic brain injury." It's an unfortunate choice of words. To qualify as a traumatic brain injury, a person's brain functioning must be altered, and there's nothing mild about that!

To further muddy the waters, every brain responds differently. Some people will recover from truly horrific injuries while others can have lifelong effects from less serious ones. There appears to be a cumulative effect. As we're seeing in former NFL players, a third, fourth, or fifth concussion can have catastrophic consequences. Certainly, Martha's age was a factor too. In another peculiar turn of phrase, doctors say the human brain is plastic and can repair itself.[8]

Until fairly recently, medical science believed our brains stopped growing and changing about the same time our bodies did. They thought that by the time we reached adulthood, we had all the brain cells we were ever going to get, but that turned out to be untrue. Our brains can continue to change throughout our lives, which is wonderful, but they do lose plasticity over time.

Finally, I told Tina, the full effect of traumatic brain injuries can sometimes take years to develop. She shot me a wry look.

---

8   Doctors aren't saying we're cheaply made. They're taking the word's original usage—as a description of something that can be shaped and reshaped. A plastic bottle is more bendable than glass.

"You know she's almost eighty, right? If it takes enough years, we may be okay." She laughed, but her smile didn't stick.

"There can be a range of these invisible injuries," I told Tina. "Other things that, like your mom's loss of executive function, don't show up on brain scans. There can be mood and behavioral changes, and those often get worse over time. The spouses of former NFL players have reported their husbands got progressively more hostile years after leaving the sport, and it wasn't because their outlook on life had changed. It's just the progression of the injuries their brains sustained with helmet-to-helmet contact while they were blocking, tackling, or slammed to the ground.

"The science behind it is clear, but don't expect the lawyers for the other side to accept it. It's going to be essential to find open-minded jury members who are willing to reconsider what they think they know, people who will listen to the experts."

Actions Speak Louder Than Words

"You know what really gets me?" Tina asked. "That the store advertises itself as 'Your friendly, neighborhood grocery store.' Not so friendly now, are they?"

The grocery store had claimed to be both friendly and local but proved to be neither. It was part of a large chain, and although it was always happy to welcome customers to spend money, its lawyers were downright hostile to us. It didn't act like a good neighbor would. In addition to finding jurors open-minded enough to learn from doctors about how trauma affects the brain, I also wanted to screen for exactly the common-sense morality Tina was pointing out that the store lacked.

When I questioned potential witnesses, I asked about what process they go through before they trust someone. I also asked how they judge a person's character or predict what someone they know might do next. A few of them quoted the old aphorism, "Actions speak louder than words," but they all said some version of the same thing. They paid more attention to what people did than what they said. When a person said one thing but did something contradictory, jurors viewed behavior as the more accurate indicator of character. I knew this would be the theme I built Martha's case around. For all its "friendly, local" branding, the store's actions spoke only of its desire for expediency, profits, and disregard for people. The store used words to attract people in, but their actions spoke volumes of what they cared about, and safety was not even near the top of the list.

Hypocrisy

In the same way that betrayal plays a role in almost every case, hypocrisy is almost always a factor. Every one of the defendants you've met in this book had a company policy or advertising slogan that, had they followed their claimed principles, would have prevented a tragedy. The defective lathe manufacturer ran a factory decorated with "Safety First!" posters but ignored that principle when designing the machines they sold. The nursing home where Rachel's mom, Ruth. died from bedsores advertised "quality, personalized elder care" where there was neither quality nor care for her. It's something I always point out to juries. I contrast what the companies say about safety and responsibility with the behaviors that caused a death or serious injury and their attempts to duck the consequences.

Character counts. We assess a person or a corporation's character by their actions. When companies only pay lip service to integrity, responsibility, and safety, people get hurt or killed. Corporate hypocrisy interrupts the life story of hundreds of people every day. When it does, they depend on our justice system to help them pick up the broken strands of that narrative and write—if not a happy, at least a just, ending.

CHAPTER 9

Dreams Never Die

Samir loaded the heavy boxes of books onto the hand truck and rolled it toward the bank of three elevators. He'd been hired for the weekend to help move an advertising agency from a beautiful old building to a sleek new one before the old one was torn down. The guy hiring him had warned that there were a lot of books, but Samir wasn't afraid of hard work. He asked what floor they were moving out of and into (the second and the third) and whether there'd be an elevator (only in the first building). He took the job. He was young and in great shape, and he needed the money.

Samir emptied bookcase after bookcase all morning, packing books into boxes, stacking boxes six high on a hand truck, and backing into the elevator for the short trip down. The doors to the center one were broken and didn't close, but the elevator car still operated, running up and down, ignored by everyone else.

Samir backed into it, keeping the hand truck slanted on the ride down and as he walked around the building to the cargo van in the alley. He always took the middle elevator back up so it would be waiting for him when he'd packed and stacked another six boxes.

He worked steadily. The guy hadn't been kidding—there were *a lot* of books. He made twelve trips back and forth. On the thirtieth, the elevator car was gone. Someone had called it to another floor. When Samir backed into the open shaft, he fell two stories breaking every bone in both feet. The impact tore ligaments from bone in his legs and blew out five disks in his spine.

Samir was in the ICU for a week and in the hospital for six additional weeks, enduring multiple surgeries, including the fusion of three of his vertebrae. His leg muscles were so severely damaged that he had to work for months to strengthen them before starting to learn to walk again—something the spinal fusions made very difficult.

The Human Spine

Our backbones are a marvel of engineering. They may be as significant in our evolution as the opposable thumb. Unlike apes, we walk on two feet, freeing our hands to carry, throw, and reach. Still, our brain communicates with our feet in milliseconds. The nerves that make this (and so much else) possible leave the brain and travel down our bodies, branching and dividing from a central column. This critical bundle of nerve fibers is protected by a stacked set of rather complicated bones called vertebrae.

A vertebra looks a bit like the face of a bull. The ears, horns, and snout form the bumps you can feel through the skin of your back while the dome of the bull's head sits almost like a full circle above, facing into your torso. Between the flattened round top of the bull's face and its spiky bottom, there's a triangular hole at about third eye level through which the spinal column runs.

The vertebrae stack one on top of another to allow us to move our torsos and create enough space between the bones for nerves to reach out from the central column to bring feeling and send movement signals to every part of our body.

Nowhere in a healthy body does bone rest directly on bone. In most places, bones are connected with cartilage, but between the large bones of your thigh and shin and between the round top portion of your vertebrae, your body creates some cushioning between bones. In your back, these pads need to be hard enough not to burst but soft enough to work as a buffer to the bones. Our bodies have cleverly solved this problem using the same technique bakers do. Like a filled doughnut, the discs between your vertebrae are made of a relatively tough "dough" filled with a soft, shock-absorbing "jelly."

The impact of Samir's fall slammed his vertebrae down one on top of the other, compacting them. It popped three "doughnuts" and forced the "jelly" out of the disks that cushioned the bones of his back. This kind of injury is called a "herniated disk" because the word "hernia" literally means "extending beyond." (In the familiar hernia often caused by lifting, it's a bit of intestine that extends beyond the abdominal muscles.)

HERNIATED DISKS

A herniated disk can cause anything from mild irritation to excruciating pain, depending on how badly it was damaged and whether the "jelly" comes in contact with the spinal nerves. When a disk is too damaged, a surgeon will often remove it, fill the gap with a plug made of metal or bone taken either from a cadaver or from the injured person's hip, and fuse the vertebrae on either side with metal bars held in place with screws.

This is what happened to Samir. The "jelly" had been pushed out from the disk and into the nerves touching the spinal column causing him chronic and unremitting pain with any movement. Sharp, stabbing, electrical pain shot from the nerves in his back down his leg. He lost all feeling in his big toe. The pain was simply relentless.

Chronic Pain

Being in constant pain changes a person. Think back to the last time you had a severe headache—were you less patient? More difficult to be around? Chronic pain can eat away at a person the way a constant drip of water erodes stone.

The corrosive effects of chronic pain aren't limited to the injured person. Their spouse, kids, families, and community suffer with them as the person they once knew and loved becomes distorted by the constant pressure of waking up every day in pain that will likely only get worse.

When I visited Samir a year after his last surgery, it was difficult to imagine struggling to reduce pain with medication and physical therapy for the entire twelve months. He was finally to a point where the good days outnumbered the bad days, but there were still too many bad days.

"I used to jump out of bed each morning," he told me. "Now, every time I wake up, I wonder what I'm going to have to face."

Samir used to go about his day without any forethought. He did not think ahead if the building he was going to had stairs to climb or how far the parking lot was from the entrance. Now, all activities required him to plan because too much in a day guaranteed the next would be one of the bad ones.

To make matters worse, insurance company lawyers had been harassing him, following him around and videotaping him as he walked across a parking lot or went into a store to pick up medicine.

"I don't know what they're trying to prove," he told me. "I'm not claiming to be paralyzed, even though I kind of wonder if I'd be better off that way. Feeling nothing would have to be better than feeling the way I do sometimes. But just because I don't let it keep me locked in the house all the time, they think there's nothing's wrong. It's not like pain is something they can see! I didn't do anything to deserve being spied on. And I know they think I'm stupid. How could I just forget the elevator was broken?"

It was a reasonable question and one I knew the jury would likely have as well. To answer it and explain the nature of Samir's back injury, we would need several different expert witnesses.

Expert Witnesses

There are almost as many kinds of expert witnesses as there are kinds of injury, but the types we most frequently call on are human factors experts, biomechanics experts, physician experts, life care planning experts, occupational therapy experts, vocational rehabilitation experts, and codes and regulatory experts.

HUMAN FACTORS

In Samir's case, I planned to bring in someone highly trained and good at explaining the way people interact with their surroundings.

Human factors experts can talk a jury through why a person at a grocery store might slip on a puddle that would have been visible on the floor. In familiar settings, we rarely glance down at the ground. In a grocery store where shelves are packed with stimuli, focusing on finding what we're shopping for, we're functionally blind to the floor we walk on. This is why reasonable care requires wet floors to be identified with an attention-getting sign or cones or marked out with tape until the spill is cleaned up.

Human factors experts can also help juries understand why a single, oddly spaced step can be extremely hazardous. Our bodies are habituated to a standard riser height and make automatic calculations about where and how to place our feet. A taller- or shorter-than-standard step, or an unmarked step a person isn't expecting, will almost always cause them to trip. Tripping on the way up a stair can cause falls, but tripping on even a single step down can cause serious injury because of the way our bodies distribute our weight. This is the reason irregularities in the floor of a public place need to be marked with reflective tape or called to your attention some other way.

In Samir's case, a human factors expert would explain to the jury how repeating an action multiple times shifts from our conscious to subconscious execution—like the way you can drive home from work on "autopilot," anything you do repeatedly gets automatically moved by your mind from the center of your active attention to its sidelines.

This feature of the human mind causes the value of posted warning signs to diminish over time until they're virtually invisible. Samir wasn't stupid or careless. After twelve repetitions with the elevator exactly where it should have been, it was scientifically reasonable and predictable that he would not check for the elevator car the thirteenth time before backing a hand truck into it.

A human factors expert was also instrumental in Ottie's case, explaining why she and Joe had eventually stopped noticing the propped open security door and burned-out lights. Our brains notice what's different, not what's stayed the same. The more we're exposed to something, the less we notice it.

BIOMECHANICS

A biomechanics expert is trained in the many ways our bodies move and what happens to them when our normal movement is disrupted. These experts have studied and can explain how the alternating stacked disks and bones of a spine allow for turning and bending. When several vertebrae are fused, the torque and strain of that movement transfer to the closest unfused disks.

It was crucial to help Samir's jury understand not only the damage already done to his spine but how that damage would impact his future. The biomechanics expert who testified at his trial explained the risk of traumatic arthritis and how the added wear and tear on his remaining disks might require Samir to undergo additional surgeries in the future.

PHYSICIANS

We almost always invite the doctors who treated the injured or killed person to explain the damage that was done and what they did to help. If additional surgeries were needed later, we often ask those doctors as well. In Samir's case, the surgeon who fused three of his vertebrae did an outstanding job explaining the procedure to the jury, detailing both what she did and the positive and negative impact it had (and would keep having) on Samir.

Physicians also explain the mechanism of injury. Jurors always want to know the way different forces impact the human body. Physicians can explain how the impact of a truck on a child's body can be fatal even at low speeds and why a father who appeared to be out of the woods could die suddenly overnight. In Samir's case, the surgeon talked the jury through how the impact of his fall traveled from his shattered feet, up his legs to his spine, driving his vertebrae one into the next with enough force to burst several of the disks designed to cushion the space between the bones.

LIFE CARE PLANNING

I ask jurors to predict my injured clients' future needs and vote for a verdict that ensures they have the funds to cover them. Experts in life care planning (also called doctors of rehabilitative medicine) are experts on what a patient's future medical needs are and what they're likely to cost. They're able to talk about when a home health aide is appropriate and discuss the need for future surgeries or additional rehabilitation. They can also speak to pain management and explain why, for some, the pain never stops.

OCCUPATIONAL THERAPY

Despite its name, occupational therapy doesn't focus on returning people to their occupations. Occupational therapists focus on the activities required in ordinary, daily life.[9] They'll often do home visits to watch people doing (or trying to do) the things they need to, like washing dishes or getting dressed. They're then able to make recommendations about which modifications and strategies the injured person requires to function as well as possible, given their new constraints.

Expert occupational therapists help juries understand how much work is required to live something approaching an ordinary life after a catastrophic injury. They can also explain the different kinds of adaptive tools they've recommended so that juries understand the ongoing expenses involved.

VOCATIONAL REHABILITATION

Vocational rehabilitation therapists specialize in helping people get back to work. Most people don't have jobs waiting for them after the year or more they've spent in hospitals and nursing or rehabilitation facilities. Experts in vocational rehabilitation therapy talk to the jury about a person's work options—whether they're capable of returning to their old job or need to have certain accommodations made for them.

Suppose an injured person can't return to what they used to do. In that case, a vocational therapist can explain how much earning capacity they've lost and what kind of job they might be able to perform. These experts also understand (and can explain) the many biases and obstacles people with disabilities face trying to get work.

Even though Samir could no longer do heavy physical work, he

9   ADLs are activities of daily living, and occupational therapist specialize in providing strategies for the seriously injured on how to accomplish their ADLs; for example, how Samir with a fused low back and get his socks on.

faced no obvious barrier to getting a desk job. Unfortunately, his chronic pain made it difficult for him to concentrate. Additionally, the longer he sat, the worse the pain got, requiring him to take frequent breaks to shift position or do a set of stretches.

In one case, we needed an expert vocational rehabilitation therapist to explain the career-ending impact the loss of a pinky finger had on a professional concert pianist. She had become a music teacher and had taken up guitar, but her income had dropped from $180,000 a year to $60,000.

CODES AND REGULATIONS

Because the defendants in our cases have so frequently violated safety regulations or ignored building codes, codes and regulatory experts are among the ones we call on most. When a tire thrown from a truck killed David, it was this kind of expert who helped the jury understand the purpose of the regulations the company had bypassed and how easy it would have been for them to do what they were supposed to that would have saved David's life.

We've also called on building code and highway safety experts, architects, product manufacturing experts, and people trained in something called "the foreseeable misuse" of products.

Strategic Trial Tools

VISUAL AIDS

We often support these experts with illustrations, diagrams, and animations to help juries visualize what the expert is telling them. We've had animators recreate a car crash and model surgical procedures. Animations make things more real for jury members and help the experts tell a compelling story.

The three most common types of animations are ones of the event that cause the injury or death (the truck driver's obstructed view, the movement of the lane-crossing bus); animations of the mechanism of injury (how the brain strikes the inside of the skull, rebounds and hits the opposite side causing damage in two places); and animations of surgical procedures.

Samir's surgeon used animation to show jurors how she cut into his back, moved major arteries out of the way, inserted an artificial disk between his vertebrae, and then drove metal screws into the bones of his back to hold them immobilized. She was able to point out risk factors—different ways Samir might have died or been paralyzed during the surgery—and underscore what a dangerous operation he had endured trying to alleviate his pain. It helped show the absurdity of the defense's argument that Samir wasn't suffering badly.

JOURNALISTS' BIOGRAPHIES

Expert witnesses supply jurors with detailed information and help them understand many of the technical details of what caused a wrongful death or catastrophic injury. They explain results and predict some outcomes. But they aren't the best-qualified people to speak to the soul of a case. The power and responsibility of a jury are to determine what comes next for the people involved; and to understand people, we need not facts or explanations, but stories.

My law firm employs expertly trained journalists to help us tell the stories of the people who have been affected by the loss of life or grave injury. One interviewed the members of Lily's church and school groups and spoke with people across four states who had known Rachel's mother. They read online obituaries and contact people who've left remembrances. They collect the family stories and little details that help paint a complete picture of the person, family, and community whose future will be shaped by the jury's verdict.

The biographers create compelling and emotional portraits that give jurors insight into everything from Martha's personality before her TBI to the number of kids Ottie was an auntie to. From Frank's old army buddies, the biographer collected stories that were inspiring and funny, and the biographer's story helped Carlos's jury feel his children's loss. Samir's biographer helped us understand the devastating impact of waking up every morning in terrible pain and illustrated how it steadily eroded Samir's physical and emotional health, his relationships, and his quality of life.

FOCUS GROUPS

In addition to experts, journalists, and animations, I have one additional resource I call on when preparing to go before a jury. I don't want to guess at what's important to them; I want to know with as much certainty as I can get. With focus groups, I test everything—the expert witnesses, my opening and closing statements, the questions I'll ask my client, and their answers. I do this preparation (at considerable expense) out of deep respect for the members of the jury and the important work they've undertaken in service to their community and our system of government.

Juries and Story

Our democracy and legal system empower their citizens with profound decision-making authority, trusting them to make heartfelt decisions based on facts, so we must speak to both their emotions and their mind. In this book, I hope you've experienced the power stories have to carry information and feeling. In a trial, lawyers carry that power into the courtroom. They bring logic to the story of fault and passion to a client's tale of loss and survival. The jury both knows and feels the truth of those stories because we also bring our souls. Trial lawyers must have credibility for a jury to accept their stories as true. Logic, passion, and credibility are the center of every trial and every story. We told Samir's story of overcoming obstacles and never giving up on his dreams to the jury, but while it was deliberating, the insurance company preemptively made an eight-figure, record-setting offer which he accepted. We rely on our clients' stories to reach the people of their juries, and we all rely on juries to write the American story.

The End (and Beginning) of Our Story

I've been very fortunate in my career to see so many good endings written for my clients by either a great settlement or jury verdict. Ottie's jury returned a verdict that taught large housing complexes that the life of every person living on their property has value. It wrote a final chapter that restored her dignity and gave meaning to Joe's death. Once the insurance company knew Ottie would only settle on her terms, they capitulated, and the case was settled.

The jury in Ruby's case delivered a strong statement to trucking companies about their responsibility to prevent the predictable. In the absence of their repentance, it gave Ruby closure in the form of their punishment.

For Franco and the rest of Lily's family, the tragic story of her death was only made more painful by the insurance company's cruel tactics of polarizing the case. They tried to blame Lily's death on her grieving mother and implied that her brother was only in it for the money.

The jury saw through their frivolous defense to the broken heart of Lily's story, and it wrote a final chapter of compassion for the family and accountability for the home services company. Her death, like the Bunbun tattoo, will mark that family for the rest of their lives. But that little rabbit's symbolic power, like that of the jury's verdict, offers an equally enduring hope.

For Martina and her children, the jury wrote the final chapter of Carlos' wrongful death, one that preserved his life's work of providing more opportunities for his boys than he'd had. But without our legal system's practice of contingent payment, it's a story we would never have been able to tell.

In the larger, ongoing story of American democracy and justice, my father's story of a courtroom with two doors needs and deserves our protection. Large corporations and their insurance companies are trying to rewrite it. I have faith that, without heart or truth on their side, they will fail. Still, I will continue to advocate for that story and for justice to be accessible to all.

In the Introduction to this book, I described myself as a deterrence lawyer—a counselor of people engaged in the hero's work of standing up to large companies who betray our trust and hypocritically talk about safety while acting with greed, indifference, or arrogance. My clients never expected to be partners in these acts of public service until the unthinkable happened. Each, like Rachel (who allowed us to bring a class-action lawsuit in the name of other people's parents), and like the other clients whose stories you've read, acted to protect other spouses, children, pedestrians, workers, drivers, and cyclists.

All of these brave people, in their own way, created a new and often better life for themselves after a jury closed the book on a wrongful death or catastrophic injury case. For Ty, the car crash that took his leg returned a new and visceral connection to his city and its people with the jury's verdict.

Having briefly despaired, Ty took heart from the process and carried what he'd learned into his education and songwriting. He came to see (as I hope you have) that even stories as widely accepted as the one claiming that in rear-end wrecks, the fault always lies with the driver in back can be wrong. He questioned that narrative, and I hope you will too. Whenever you've done all that was possible, when there are no good options, the story hasn't ended until blame and accountability are placed where it belongs.

Blame rarely belongs entirely with the individual victim, which is why we always put people first. In how our intake and investigative processes are structured, through how we tell our clients' stories to a jury, to the fraction of those stories I've shared here, people, including you, come first—before insurance company lawyers and before calculations of profit or loss.

My commitment to putting people first is part of the reason I'm donating all the proceeds from the sale of this book. My mother was an extraordinary person who offered help and hope to people in our community. Doing the same by telling client stories of justice and recovery for people I'll likely never meet is part of her legacy, so it seems only fitting that any profits that come from it be directed back toward the work she supported. I was young when she died, but I know who she was because of what she did.

Actions prove identity. It's why a traumatic brain injury that changes how a person acts alters who they are. It's why corporate hypocrisy creates such dissonance. It's how we read something powerfully affirming about our fellow Americans in the decisions of our juries.

Juries write the last chapter on stories of tragedy and help grieving and injured people turn them into the first chapters of triumph over hardship. I hear so many stories of heartbreak and despair that I couldn't keep doing my job if I didn't believe that juries generally do the right thing and that clients can always write new stories for their lives after we part ways.

No one is ever happy to need a lawyer like me, but I hope that by the time we finish working together, they're glad we met. I hope if you're reading this book because your life has been upended by a death or injury that you've gained some hope for an eventually positive outcome. I hope you have a better understanding of the role the justice system might play in helping bring it about. I wish you strength and courage and eventual closure and peace. If you're reading for any other reason, I wish you well.

I hope we never meet.